About The Author

Sandra personally suffered from Systemic Candida for over 10 years, barely holding it at bay with prescribed medication. In 2010 it came to a head and she decided that conventional medicine wasn't working for her – she chose to heal herself through her diet (alongside a natural treatment plan).

This book is the result of all her research, trial and error, testing what works and what doesn't – all with the help and feedback from the thousands of subscribers to her Blog, Newsletter and Facebook community over the past 4 years.

So let her guide you on your journey to health and vitality through 100% wholesome & tasty food! It's worked for her and many others, and she truly believes it can work for you too!

Key to Abbreviations

Naturally all the recipes in this book are **free of refined sugars, yeast and processed foods or artificials.**

Most recipes are also gluten free and dairy free. The dairy in the few recipes that do contain **dairy can easily be replaced with a dairy-free alternative.** *For instance tempeh/ tofu instead of feta/ cottage cheese and rice/ almond/ coconut milk instead of goats milk and unsweetened soy yogurt instead of sheep or goats.*

Regarding common allergens: Whereever possible I give **egg free alternatives** within the recipe, and I don't use Soya. There are only 3 recipes with **nuts** and these are marked (contains nuts). Shellfish recipes always name a **shellfish free alternative.** And with most meat dishes I give a vegetarian option.

The recipes are naturally **sugar, sweetener & grain free** like most soups, salads, meat, fish and vegetarian meals.

The abbreviations after each recipe title indicate which recipes are gluten free (gf), dairy free (df), and vegan (v) (*which would include dairy free and egg free*).

Since the sweetness of the meals is very important to Candida sufferers I have also **included references to what sweeteners the recipes contain (S) Stevia (X) Xylitol**. The vast majority of recipes is without any sweetener though.

Hearty mains generally contain no abbreviations. For instance Roast Chicken is naturally (GF) &(DF), but I don't mention this specifically. So please read through the ingredients's list to double-check that the meal doesn't contain anything that you might be allergic or sensitive to.

(GF) - Gluten free
(DF) - Dairy free
(V) - Vegan (dairy & egg free)

Table of Contents

DINNER RECIPES

DESSERTS

HEALTHY SNACKS

Intro

Hi my name is Sandra, and I'd like to welcome you to the start of your journey to health!

I am thrilled you picked up this book and decided to try out some of my low carbs recipes – that's awesome!

Judging by the positive feedback I've been getting from the 20 dedicated recipes testers you'll find some new go-to recipes in here that will make your life a lot easier. If you follow the provided meal plan you should also see an improvement in your health and how you feel.

This book is aimed at people with food sensitivities and auto-immune, digestive or chronic health issues – especially Candida. If you've never heard of Candida don't worry, it's just a sign of a low immune system most people have at one point in their life - especially after a period of taking antibiotics. You can quickly check if you have any of the symptoms by going through the checklist on my blog at http://candidadietplan.com/colon-cleanse-recipes/candida-symptoms/

If you already know about Candida then you'll be pleased to hear that it is possible to make nice tasting meals (even if you can't use cream, sugar, refined flour or cheese in your cooking!). So don't despair (at least not before you have tried my killer "Creamy Veggie Soup recipe with Crispy Turkey Strips" recipe -- that alone is worth the price of the book says my lovely reader Cat. All recipes in this book are 100% sugar and yeast free, and most are gluten and dairy free. You'll find Paleo (grain free meat, fish & egg based) meals as well as plant based meals.

If you haven't got a medical condition or you suffer from Chronic Fatigue, Diabetes, IBS or Gluten-/ Dairy intolerance you should still be able to get a lot of value out of this book. You just wouldn't have to follow the diet as strictly as a Candida sufferer would.

The majority of the recipes are quick to make: 20-30 minutes max.

BONUS: 5 NEW CANDIDA DIET RECIPES + 2 WEEK MEAL PLAN

This cookbook contains the latest up-to-date version of over 40 of the most popular Candida diet recipes from my blog candidadietplan.com including 5 completely NEW sugar free recipes and a 2 Week Meal Plan (only available as part of this book; not on the website).

I hope you'll find my recipes and comments useful,

Keep in touch!
Sandra x

How to get the most out of this book

I recommend you don't just pick a few recipes and cook them. You'll achieve much greater results if you follow the 2 week meal plan at the end of this book, and then once you're done with that, cook your way through the second recipes book in this series. The idea is to carry on with at least 2 weeks low carbs diet plan as soon as you're finished with this one.

The diet laid out in this book is called The Candida Diet and the book is divided into 2 stages (the first stage is a short cleanse/ fast; the second is two weeks of fairly strict diet).

You might have heard of the Specific Carbohydrate Diet, Atkins, Paleo or The Body Ecology Diet - these are all very similar to the Candida Diet. They limit grains and carbs intake and focus on foods that are gentle on your digestive system, helping your body heal while boosting your immune system.

Stage 1 (the fast) is optional. I have included some recipes for a nourishing broth and veggie juices just in case you want to give that a go.

These are the stages of the diet I recommend you follow:

Stage 1 - Fast (1-7 days; optional)
Stage 2 - Strict No Carbs Diet (2 weeks)

Go straight to stage 2 if you want to skip the fast.

You'll find a quick overview, plenty of recipes and a recap of what you've learned in that stage. Stage two recipes are fairly easy to digest, and because you'll be drastically limiting your carbs and gluten intake your digestive symptoms should be getting better, lowering inflammations in your entire body.

Less brain fog, more energy. You will lose a lot of weight though, and it is advised that you take some colon cleansing herbs to keep things moving (to avoid constipation), as this tends to happen when you remove fiber from your diet.

But even once you have accomplished stage 2 and you can slowly start eating carbs again it is definitely a good idea to dig out a few of these recipes again; at least whenever you are starting to feel unwell or you want to lose weight.

Originally I wanted to include recipes for all four stages of the diet here. But when I looked at the Candida diet recipes books out there I noticed that they contain mostly carbs recipes which can be confusing, as it looks like you should be allowed to eat them. But from my own experience and from my readers' I know that eating carbs during the first few weeks of the diet is really tricky. It is very easy to relapse. So I thought it would be less tempting for you if I just included "Candida safe" recipes in this book. That way there is no confusion.

A few words about Candida & My Medical Disclaimer

Basically, if you think you have Candida then you'll have to follow the diet quite strictly for several weeks if not months. You'll have to take some natural meds and probiotics to re-build your immune system. Diet is only part of the medallion.

There are good free resources on the Internet, if you want to put a treatment plan together yourself. That's what I did.

You can follow my progress along on my blog at candidadietplan.com or you can peruse my health journey and treatment plan quickly at your leisure on Amazon (just search for "The Candida Diet Solution Sandra Boehner").

That said, if you have access to a nutritionist/ digestive expert with a proven track record of healing people, then I'd definitely recommend getting professional help. You'd heal so much quicker by avoiding trial and error. Just bear in mind that what I'm sharing here with you is just from my own experience and recipes I developed for myself. I have no medical qualification and if you try out my recipes or you follow in my footsteps, this might very well not agree with you. I cannot accept any responsibility for that. You have been warned ;-)

Why I had to give up sugar

After conventional doctors had not been able to cure my health symptoms, and the naturopath had assured me the diet I was following was very wholesome, I carried on with what I thought was a "healthy" diet: fresh fruit smoothie followed by Müsli with dried fruit and semi skimmed milk for breakfast, more fruit and copious amounts of tea with manuka honey; then wholewheat bread with cheese and later wholewheat pasta with chicken and vegetables.

Since the diet was high in sugar and highly acidic, my symptoms intensified and I just "knew" that it had to do with the sugar and grains I was consuming. I started researching on the Internet and found interesting information that confirmed my suspicion.

I was able to identify that all my health problems stemmed from a yeast imbalance that was allowed to undermine my immune system for years as it had been undiscovered and therefore untreated.
It made total sense to me because even the recurring health issues that had troubled me half my life (bladder infections, yeast infections/ thrush, hayfever…, sensitivity to smoke and strong smells… were classic Candida symptoms (You can go through the free symptom check list here to see if you're affected).

By that point I had lost faith in the conventional health system I decided I might as well follow the diet that was meant to cure Candida induced health problems, since I had nothing to lose.

The Turning Point:

So I printed off some sugar and yeast free recipes I had found on the web and embarked on the Candida diet. I quickly got better, and I equally as quickly got bored of the recipes I had found.

As the yeast overgrowth had totally undermined my immune system and caused secondary infections and hormonal imbalances that weren't so easy to get rid of, it did take me a while to get fully well again. Hence I was forced to adapt recipes to my liking, not to have to eat the same old boring sugar deprived foods again and again.

I learned through trial and error, openly sharing my recipes and what natural treatments I followed on my blog candidadietplan.com. This gave me a great platform to interact with and learn from other Candida sufferers who also had chronic health issues.

This sped my recovery up no end. So much so that I got a bit cocky and relaxed the diet, enjoying lots of fruit and the odd ice cream and cocktail, reveling in how good I felt. That sadly led to a relapse and the return of some familiar health problems and discomforts, not to mention the emotional downward spiral this entailed.

But when I started to follow the diet again, it wasn't long until I got back to where I had left off. Once again seeing how powerful the diet is when followed systematically.

All throughout the long recovery from my auto-immune, respiratory and emotional health issues I kept a food diary. I have a very clear idea what meals helped me to get better and which ones weren't so beneficial.

The Feedback of Hundreds of Readers and Kind Recipes Testers Helped Shape these Recipes
I also got a lot of feedback from the hundreds of readers who followed in my footsteps, eating according to my Candida diet recipes. This gave me an abundance of healthy tasty recipes to choose from for this book. Yet I took it one step further and fed the short-listed recipes to my family and friends to make sure that they were easy enough to cook for even busy people.

It was also important to me that the recipes tasted really good to people who don't know anything about nutrition.

All the recipes in this book are staple dishes that I've been refining for over two years. I am confident that you will find one or the other new dish in here that you will permanently add to your cooking repertoire. And if you don't normally cook, then you'll be pleased to here that the dishes I'm about to show you don't require cooking skills. They are quick and easy to make.

I know how daunting it can feel to take your health into your own hands, and how it can feel confusing and as if you were tapping in the dark, not knowing what will help you. I truly hope that I can inspire you to try out a few new recipes.

Nobody expects you to change your diet completely. Just grab a big mug of tea and peruse the recipes in this book at your leisure.

Best Results When You Follow a Meal Plan

My advice for you though is to pick a week and literally plot out what you're going to eat that week. You can just copy mine, that's what it's there for ;-) or you can develop your own.

You can download the free meal plan as well as four already filled in meal plans if you sign up to my weekly newsletter: http://candidadietplan.com/4weekly-meal-plans

It is so much easier to eat healthily, when all you have to do is follow the plan. I do this every week, and it has helped me no end.

Better still (if you haven't been feeling so well for quite some time): Also Keep a Food Diary

If you currently suffer from health symptoms then you can take it even one step further: You could write a food diary. It's just a way of documenting what you've eaten on a certain date and how you felt. When you do this regularly you'll quickly see patterns that you would otherwise miss.

For instance I noticed in my food diary that my inflammations flared up after eating oats, and yet I believed that I wasn't allergic to oats and could therefore eat oats. When you keep seeing that you feel worse after eating what you regard as delicious highly nutritious breakfast, eventually you're going to try something different, right? Only because I kept a food diary and noticed the pattern I started to question the belief I had about what foods agreed with me. It's easy to turn a blind eye on something you don't want to give up.

A Few Words of Encouragement

If some foods don't agree with you at the moment, don't despair. At one point I reacted to meat, eggs, all grains (including Quinoa, millet and Buckwheat which are meant to be so allergy friendly...!) sugar, yeast, cream, milk, butter, cheese, tomatoes, mushrooms, bell peppers, garlic, beans, bread, coffee, fruit, alcohol and sweets... not to mention the hefty allergy fits I had when I so much as just thought of dust mites or pollen...!

Now I can enjoy pretty much anything (in moderation!) I am of course still a little cautious, because the last thing I want is to jeopardize my newly found wellbeing. But I can enjoy oatmeal porridge, a sweet pudding, roast chicken and even the odd pizza or a glass of wine without any problems.

Everything is possible! I want you to feel great - and not go hungry, haha :)

Tools You Need

What you normally use for cooking and baking will work just fine. I happened to have these kitchen ware items at hand, but just use what you normally would:

- A non stick Frying pan (a small one 8inch for toasting seeds or making oatmeal porridge; and a big 11inch one with cover for sautéing vegetables and cooking omelets and frittatas)
- A Stainless Steel 3 quart stack and steam saucepan (for quickly steaming vegetables and fish; and to make sauces and melt butter)
- A 12-cup muffin pan
- A non stick roast and broil pan 13 by 9 by 2 1/4 inches (to roast chicken and vegetables)
- Standard rack that sits in the grill part of the top oven (to grill fish, bacon and chicken)
- A 2 quart round casserole dish
- A 6 quart stainless steel soup pot
- A 10 by 15 inches cookie pan
- A round Quiche dish/ pie form with 1.6qt capacity 10 1/2 by 1-3/8 inches
- A non stick bread loaf pan (a medium 8.5 inch by 4 one baking gluten free breads and a 12 inch by 4 one for baking Spelt or whole-wheat flour breads)
- A 9 inch spring form pan (for baking cake) and three small ones 4 by 1 3/4 inches

When I talk about cups in the recipes I mean US cups; I try to give metric measurements as well wherever possible.

Kitchen Ingredients Essentials

You'll find that you'll already have most of the ingredients in the house: **meat, eggs, fish, olive oil, plain yogurt, vegetables (and I also recommend wholegrain rice).**

To see exactly what you need to get started, refer to the pantry list at the end of the book, and if you sign up to my newsletter at candidadietplan.com you even get a printable version of the list. The list includes the brands I like best and where I buy them. Hopefully this will help you find good suppliers where you live, too.

Other useful staples to have:

- Organic brown rice milk (or unsweetened almond or semi skimmed goats milk)

- Coconut butter/ oil - for frying and spreading on bread instead of dairy butter (although I occasionally use that too). You can get by without Coconut oil. But a little goes a long way, and it kills Candida.

- Tinned fish (sardines are better than tuna because of the mercury content, but I use both on a regular basis) - makes a great snack or lunch with a salad and boiled egg. You want to eat more oily fish, fresh and tinned - it's anti-inflammatory!

- Tinned tomatoes and tomato paste (called tomato puree in the UK)- check that these don't contain citric acid, you might have to buy this at a health food store. It's worth it though, tastes milder and is better for you. Great for making sauces and as base for pizza and hot pots.

- Sunflower and pumpkin seeds and desiccated coconut - for sprinkling on salads and breads and to snack on.

- Plenty of organic vegetables, eggs, meat and fresh fish.

- Low salt - I generally use Sea salt, garlic or onion salt, but too much sodium/ salt isn't good for you - makes your body retain water and toxins in your tissues. So Low Salt is great in that it tastes like "salt" but contains less sodium. Keep an eye out for it next time you go groceries shopping.

- Probiotic yogurt (I found sheep's yogurt the tastiest because of it is thick and creamy like Greek yogurt). But regular dairy or goats yogurt works, too. Just make sure that it's not pasteurized as this kills the goodness. Dairy can cause stomach/ gut upsets; goats tastes as if a goat breathed in your face, haha.

- A good herbal tea and if you like green tea (yes, you need to wean yourself off coffee, I'm afraid - it messes with your biorhythm and blood sugar levels). Herbal tea is even better for you than black or green tea because the fermentation process of the latter can disrupt the microflora in your gut.

- Brown (wholegrain) rice in place of white rice.

- Turmeric spice - you'll see me adding this to most of my recipes - it gives dishes a lovely yellow color with virtually no flavor yet super cancer fighting/ preventing properties.

- Almond butter - for snacking on; in moderation! ;-)

STAGE 1 -- 2 DAYS FAST

A short fast is recommended to boost your immune system.
In the first chapter I show you what broth, juice, smoothie and snacks you can have to make it easier.
Let's get started!

How long is this stage?

Anywhere from 1 day to 7 days. Most people fast for 1-2 days. Others go straight to stage 2. You achieve a deeper cleansing/ healing effect if you fast. But this can also result in you feeling worse for wear initially. If you start straight with the diet the detox reaction is generally gentler -- your choice.

What You Need to Avoid:

- Food haha… (especially meat, fried food, dairy, wheat, alcohol, coffee and sugar)
- Stress (it really is super important that you can take some time out to recuperate)

What You Need to Do:

- Drink lots of water, herbal teas, bone and veggie broth.
- If you want to do a bit of a fast but can't take time off work I'd recommend drinking veg etable broth and nibbling some veggie sticks with hummus at lunch time or an avocado.
- Slices of cucumber also help. If you are working out or very active eat something light (salads and steamed veggies with cooked brown rice or quinoa for instance).

What Not to Do:

- Avoid going for your usual shop (Your tendency will be to buy lots of stuff because you think you'll be starving soon. Then you have all this nice food in the house and can't start the fast because you have to use it all up – been there...!)
- Don't put it off because you have some appointment or family do (there never is "the ideal time for a fast") Just work your way around it. Eating brown rice, vegetables and hummus to see you through this day is better than putting off the whole fast for another week or a month...
- Resist the urge to get every superfood, cleanse and you name it product to create "the perfect cleanse experience". It will just make it harder to do and bankrupt you. Pick only what's necessary.
- It is super important not to get stressed out about the meals and the preparation. Stress is just as bad as eating sugar! So simplify your meals and your life in general.

If you have no time to cook– bulk cook things like vegetable broth and coconut rice. That frees up your time to make a vegetable juice, big salad, steam vegetables or try something new like sprouting or fermented vegetables...

If you feel overwhelmed - stop working harder, go for a 10 min walk instead or simply lie on the floor with your knees at an angle – relaxes your nervous system - try it ;-)

When you shouldn't do a fast (or at least not without medical supervision):

- when you're pregnant or breast feeding
- when you're under a lot of stress, working hard or physically very active
- when you feel weak or emotionally distressed
- when you're underweight or ill.

Overview of liquid foods & drinks you can have

Make sure you drink a lot of filtered water and any of the following nourishing drinks:

1. Fasting Tea
2. Vegetable Broth for Fasting
3. Bone Broth
4. Green Juice
5. Green Smoothie
6. Ginger Root Tea
7. Water with a dash of Apple Cider Vinegar
8. Dandelion Tea/ coffee and if you can't go without coffee try Chicoree

Nourishing & Detoxifying Drinks

Fasting Tea Pg.15

Veggie Broth Pg.16

Nourishing Bone Broth Pg.17

Green Juice Pg.18

Creamy Green Smoothie Pg.19

Tomato Basil Juice Pg.20

Ginger Root Tea Pg.57

Water & Apple Cider Vinegar Pg.57

Dandelion Tea or Chicoree Coffee substitute Pg.57&58

Fasting Tea (GF, DF, V)

Plain but with a subtle aroma this tea will be a welcome stomach soother when you can't have food!

Prep: 0　　　　**Cooking Time: 5 minutes**

Ingredients:

- Cinnamon sticks, 1 tablespoon of Aniseed (or Fennel seeds) and 6 cloves (the mint leaf in the picture above is only deco)

Here's how you make it:

- Bring 1 1/2l water to the boil and add the spices.
- Simmer the mixture for 5 minutes and leave to infuse for a bit.
- Make a flask of this Candida cleanse/ fasting tea and drink one cup every 3-4 hours.

Vegetable Broth for Fasting (GF, DF, V)

Don't expect the broth to taste delicious. It tastes rather bland to be honest. I have yet to find a fasting broth that tastes good!

Prep: 8 minutes   Cooking Time: 30 minutes

- Add a little yeast free chicken stock/ broth to make it more palatable. This is a bit naughty because during a fast you should not consume sodium/ salt as this hinders your body's ability to expel toxins. But that's what I did, and still achieved great detoxing results.
- Make a big pot that lasts you 2-3 days. Then you don't have to worry about cooking during your cleanse.

Tip: Add 1/4 tsp Spirulina powder to your broth before eating - this might look and smell a bit odd, but it gives you an energy boost (which you might be grateful for!)

Ingredients:

- 1 1/2l (1.5 quarts, 6 generous cups) filtered water
- 1 handful Broccoli
- 1 handful Cabbage
- 1 Onion
- 2 Leek
- 1 stalk Celery

Optional

- 1 handful Kale, Spinach or Asparagus

Here's how you make it:

- Boil the vegetables in 1.5 l of water for about half an hour. Now you've got 2 options:

Option 1 (tastes horrible) - You strain the broth through a sieve, disregarding the veg.
Option 2 - You spoon some of the veg back into the broth and eat that...or blend it with some spices into a thicker soup. But try not to. The thicker the soup, the more energy your body will spend on digestion rather than healing.

- Garnish with a bit of freshly chopped parsley if you have.

You can add pretty much any vegetables you like. It's only sweet & starchy vegetables that you need to be a bit cautious with (carrot, potatoes, butternut squash…). Adding a little bit of coconut milk is fine, but not ideal because it is very acidic. I definitely would also advise you not to eat coconut flesh because it is a lot of work for your digestive system. The good thing about coconut is though that it doesn't feed Candida. Rather the opposite actually. But use coconut oil sparingly if at all.

Good luck with the cleanse :)

Immune System Boosting Bone Broth (GF, DF)

Forget the name, focus on what it can do for you. It is full of nutrients that boost your health and make you more resilient to colds and infections.

Prep: 8 minutes   **Cooking Time: 3-4 hours**

Ingredients

- 1 Chicken carcass or 1lbs (500g) beef marrow bones (preferably organic)
- 2l (2 quart) of boiling water

optional:
- 2 bay leafs
- a few black pepper corns
- 1 onion
- 1 big celery stalk
- a bunch of fresh or dried herbs - add this during the last 30 minutes of cooking (parsley for instance is high in Vitamin C)
- 1 vegetable stock cube or 1 tsp of sea salt
- dash of apple cider vinegar (to break down the minerals in the bone)

Here's how you make it:

- Briefly fry the bones in a little olive oil from all sides (this enhances the flavor of the broth). Alternatively you could bake the bones in the oven for about 30 mins at 350 F, 180 C, Gas 4.
- Transfer them into a slow cooker/ crock pot or a huge pot on the hob. Pour the water over the bones/carcass, covering as much as possible, and add the Bay leaves, stock cube and peppercorns or vegetables if using.
- Cook on a medium heat for 30 minutes to an hour, then turn down to low and simmer for 3-4 hours. After an hour or so stir the bones around so all bones are covered. If necessary add more water.
- Let the broth chill. Either use up in the next couple of days or freeze in small portions

Note: Regular stock from vegetables or meat tends to simmer only a few hours, whereas bone broth simmers for 12-36 hours. This prolonged cooking time helps to get as many minerals and nutrients off the bones as possible. But unfortunately this can also cause severe die off and histamin symptoms. So in the beginning of the diet it's best to start slowly with 3-4 hours cooking time, and when you know this agrees with you extend the cooking time for maximum health benefit. This is a tip I got from my lovely reader Sarah (thank you for reminding me Sarah, if you're reading this).

Why drinking bone broth is good for you:

Bone broth is super rich in nutrients – especially acids and minerals. These support the your body's natural detoxification processes and digestion, by positively impacting bile flow and stomach function. It also help heal skin problems because the gelatin that it contains improves collagen which is essential for a healthy skin. Gelatin also plays an important role in the healing the leaky gut problem that is common in people with chronic allergies and digestive problems.

Green Juice (GF, DF, V)

Now here's a drink that tastes pretty awful (sorry! I DO have your best interests at heart, honestly!)

I had to include this drink because it is a real vitamin & mineral powerhouse (despite its taste!) So be strong and just drink this whenever you need a little something.

Prep: 3 minutes   Time to make: 1 minute

Ingredients

- 1 handful fresh spinach or watercress leaves
- 1 handful basil, parsley or coriander (cilantro)
- half a large organic cucumber
- 1-2 stalks celery
- juice of 1 lemon

Optional

- 1 clove garlic
- 1/4 tsp each of Spirulina and Chlorella powder

Note (Helpful to Beat Cravings!):

Try lime instead of lemon for a slightly sweeter flavour. Green juices are superb immune system boosters - They do however take a little getting used to. Try one at least once though. The main thing is that the juice gives you lots of energy and helps you to keep your cravings at bay. During your fast this can be a real life-saver. Put the greens, cucumber celery and finely chopped garlic (if using) into a juicer to make a green liquid. Juice the lemon and mix in with your green juice. Don't worry if you leave out the garlic, it's pretty poky. The juice is still very good for you even without.

Stir in some Spirulina and Chlorella for an extra health boost. It's helpful to remove heavy metals from your body Heavy metal poisoning can cause all sorts of health issues and you might have raised levels without even realizing. Typical culprits are Teflon frying pans, dental fillings and tuna. But don't stop eating tuna now please. Just make sure you eat a wide variety of fish; sardines for instance contain less mercury than tuna.

Keep the rest of your juice in a covered jar in the fridge and drink as soon as possible. It might be worth getting a proper juice flask if you drink a lot of juices. These are dark bottles made out of a thermos flask-type material that keep the vitamins fresh for longer.

Quick Alternative to Green Juice

A glass of water with a tip of a tsp of spirulina, double the amount of chlorella, barley grass or wheat grass powder and a dash of freshly pressed lemon juice (and you don't even need a juicer for this!)

Creamy Green Calmer Smoothie (GF, DF, V)

The cashew nuts make this smoothie extra sweet & creamy.

Prep: 2 minutes   **Time to make: 1 minute**

Ingredients:

- 5 Lettuce leaves
- ½ Cucumber
- handful of Spinach
- 1/4 tsp Chlorella
- 1/4 tsp Spirulina
- handful of Cashew nuts
- ½ can chilled creamy Coconut milk
- dash of Rice milk

optional: handful of fresh coriander, basil or mint leaves

Here's how you make it:

Simply blend all the ingredients until you have a thick creamy smoothie. The name says it all – this smoothie really calms you down. And if it brings a moment of calm to your day, that can only be good, right ;-)Now I could tell you that that's because of the *soporific* qualities of the lettuce. But let's just say that once you experience the *silky sweet smoothness* of this coconutty creation, you'll forget all finer details any way…

One word of warning though (best kept to a minimum during the fast):

- Sensitive individuals might react to the Cashew nuts in the snoothie. If that's the case with you try swapping them for almonds or just leave them out.

- Another thing to bare in mind that the thicker a smoothie is the harder it is to digest and the more energy it takes your body to do that. That's why it's recommended during a fast to drink juices rather than smoothies – to reserve all energy for cleansing and healing. But as I know that there might be moments during your fast when you need a little more than just a green juice or broth, I've included the smoothie here for you. Just in case ;-) As long as you only have it when you're starving or you're snowed under with work/ stress, you should be fine.

Tomato & Basil Pick me up (GF, DF, V)

Here's a lovely juice that helps to lift your mood up during a fast or candida cleanse program.

I've never been a great fan of vegetable juices myself; let alone tomato juices.
But as this juice is simple, sweet and refreshing I'm happy to share it with you.

Prep: 1 minute   Time to make: 1 minute

Ingredients

- 6 ripe Tomatoes on the vine
- 1 handful fresh basil leaves
- a sprinkle salt & freshly ground black pepper
- a sprinkle of garlic granules

Here's how you make it:

Wash the tomatoes and basil leaves. Then whizz them up together in a food blender or smoothie maker. Enjoy as it is or add a sprinkle of spice to it.

Two snacks that require no prep time:

- **Chilled Cucumber Slices**

Used in Ayurvedan traditions; no calories and very soothing.

Last but not least, it's always helpful to have a few slices of chilled cucumber at hand. I know it sounds odd. But it is a fantasticly healthy snack during a cleanse.

- **Avocados**

Healthiest snack food ever.

Good for your skin and nerves and a total life saver during a fast when you need that extra bit of energy to tame your cravings (especially if you can't take time off work or have family responsibilities dropped on you last minute).

RECAP OF STAGE 1

Awesome, you've decided to get healthier! Thumbs up from me.

Have you had a chance to do a fast? If you did, marvelous - this will really kick-start your health. If you want to jump straight into the diet, that's fine, too. This is your health

journey. Do what's best for you.

STAGE 2 -- 2 WEEKS (PROTEIN MEALS)

In this chapter you'll learn how to use protein rich meals to lose weight (should you wish to) and to cut out carbs (sugar) & grains to heal your digestive system.

STRICT NO CARBS DIET

The Idea of this Stage is to avoid eating anything that

- *feeds Candida*
- *and anything that could cause an allergic reaction*
- *or anything that causes indigestion*

Key is

- *To eat light*
- *Get as many vitamin & minerals as possible*
- *To improve digestion & support your liver, kidneys and adrenals*
- *Use natural remedies like teas and herbs to make you feel better*
- *It is super important not to get stressed out about the meals and the preparation. Stress is just as bad as eating sugar!*
- *So simplify your meals and your life in general.*
- *Only embark on this journey if you think you're body is in a fit state to do so.*

Just like in Stage 1 it is very important here that you are not pregnant, ill or underweight to begin with, as you'll lose weight and could end up malnourished and get infections. If in doubt, ask your doctor.

Remember, changing one's eating habits is a big step.
But if you strive to live just a little bit healthier every week you'll be amazed what you can achieve!

Stay with it. You've made a fantastic start, and you're not alone!

I suggest for the next two weeks you rotate between the following recipes:

- Creamy Coconut Rice
- Veggy Omelet
- Poached Cod with Cherry Tomatoes

Simple Slimming Meals

Creamy Coconut Rice
Pg.23

Quick Omelet
Pg.24 & 36

Poached Cod
Pg.25

Bone Broth
Pg.17/26

Chicken Soup
Pg.27

Cauliflower & Almond Soup
Pg.28

Kale & Roast Meat Soup
Pg.29

Grilled Chicken Salad
Pg.30

Salad Nicoise
Pg.31

Indian Scrambled Eggs
Pg.32

Sardines & Boiled Eggs
Pg.33

Grain Free Paleo Pie Crust
Pg.34

BREAKFAST RECIPES

Creamy Coconut Rice (GF, DF, V)

Slow release energy food & good for your nerves.

But stick to one small bowl for now, chew every bite really slowly, and don't have rice every day. You really want to cut down on Carbs as much as possible. Naturally this tastes a little bland, you're on a diet, right! Rest assured -- there'll be tastier foods to come ;-)

Prep: 1 minute   Cooking Time: 35-40 minutes

Ingredients:

- 1/2 cup or more (60g Brown Rice)
- 1 tablespoon Coconut Oil
- 1 pinch Cinnamon

Optional: 1 tablespoon of de-shelled hemp seeds or ground sunflower and pumpkin or chia seeds for extra nutrition (drink more liquid because the chia seeds swell up in your tummy)

Here's how you make it:
Bring 1 l (1 quart) of water to the boil. Add a little bit of salt. Cook the washed rice in the simmering water for 35 minutes or until soft, stirring frequently. The softer the rice, the nicer the taste (to me anyway; you might prefer it more al dente!) Add more water if the rice is starting to stick to the bottom of the pan.

Strain the cooked rice through a big sieve and put it back into the sauce pan. Stir in the Coconut oil and serve immediately as it loses heat quickly. Add cinnamon & seeds if you like. Great as breaky or as a snack.

You might be wondering "If week 2 and 3 are *'no carbs'*, how can we have rice?"

This is a valid question. The idea is not to eat any carbs during this phase. But most people find that impossible and encounter insane cravings, anxiety and depression, which then might lead to a relapse into eating sugary foods out of frustration or it might severely impact their ability to work. People also tend to starve themselves when they start the diet and end up not taking in enough nutrients, which in turn slows their healing down.

Brown rice is easy to digest, rich in minerals, keeps the blood sugar stable and with it's B vitamins also supports the nerves in this time of extreme stress. The little natural sugar in it gets released into the blood stream very slowly, especially combined with green vegetables or in combination with the antifungal action of coconut oil and cinnamon. Rice also promotes regularity which is so important in the fight against Candida. All in all the benefits outweigh the negative aspects in my opinion. Refined white rice and big amounts are off the books of course. But eating a little bit of unsweetened brown rice every now and again is not going to sabotage your recovery. I personally found it a godsend, and did not experience any problems from eating it at all. And I know that it has helped a lot of my readers, too. Hope this has clarified things a little :-)

Quick Omelet with Green Pepper and Leek (GF, DF)

Super quick and very versatile.

Try it with different veggies (for instance tomato and basil with or without tuna) and have it regularly. Best to make double the amount for the next day.

Prep: 3 minutes   Cooking time: 10 minutes

Ingredients:

- 2-3 Eggs
- 1 Green Bell Pepper (yes -- Green! Red peppers naturally contain more sugar hence they are less)
- 1 Small Leek
- 1/2 tsp Salt & freshly ground Black Pepper
- 1/4 tsp Turmeric (Kurkuma)
- 1 handful Pine Kernels (optional)
- 1 handful Fresh Basil or Spinach Leaves (chopped finely)

Version 1: Quickly fried on the hob

Here's how you make it:

- Lightly chop and sauté the leek and bell pepper in a little olive oil with Turmeric and salt and pepper until soft and golden. Then break the eggs into a bowl and blend with a fork. Briefly mix in the sautéd vegetables.
- Add half a teaspoon of butter to the frying pan. Then pour the egg leek mix back into the frying pan to cover the entire base (6 inches/ 15cm).
- Season with salt and pepper and add the chives or basil if using. Roast the pine kernels lightly in a small frying pan and sprinkle over the top of the omelet if using. Now you can also sprinkle any herbs or spinach over the Omelet.
- Sauté until it sets and you can move a spatula underneath the omelet. Make sure it doesn't stick to the frying pan when you turn it to sauté the other side lightly. Serve with a green salad.

Version 2: Gently baked in the oven

Well worth a try, looks very pretty and you can get on with other stuff while it's bubbling away in the oven - Nice!

Prep: 3 minutes   Cooking time: 30-35 minutes

- Preheat the oven to 190°C/fan170°C/gas5. Brush a 20cm round pie form with olive oil or cooking spray.
- You still lightly sauté the veggies and separately whisk and season the eggs as before.
- But you fill the pie form with the veggies and just pour the eggs on top, making sure it spreads evenly. Again, sprinkle any spinach or basil leaves or pine kernels you have on top and bake on. Bake for 30-35 minutes, or until the top is slightly golden and a knife inserted in the middle comes out clean. Let cool for 5 minutes before slicing. Take out of the fridge some time before serving to bring the flavours out.

Poached Cod with Cherry Tomatoes (GF, DF)

This dish works nicely as a lunch or dinner option.

But it is mainly used as a filling Candida Diet breakfast recipe during Stage 2 of the diet when no bread or cereal are allowed.

Prep: 2 minutes   Cooking time: 10 minutes

Ingredients:

- 1 piece fresh Cod
- 5 ripe Cherry Tomatoes (whole)
- 2 heaped tablespoons Tomato paste (tomato puree in the UK)
- 1 clove Garlic (finely chopped)
- pinch salt & black pepper
- rice – or goat's milk (enough to almost cover the fish, about 150-300 ml/ 0.6- 1.2 cups)

Optional:

- 1 handful fresh Spinach or Basil leaves
- 1-2 teaspoon ground Arrowroot (for thickening the sauce)
- 1 pinch Curry Spice

Here's how you make it:

- Put the fish into a deep frying pan and add enough milk to cover the base of the pan. Sprinkle your seasoning on top of the fish. Bring to the boil and occasionally pour some of the goat's/ rice milk onto the fish to cook it evenly. (If using frozen fish, let it defrost for at least half a day before processing).

- Add the tomato paste, the washed tomatoes (whole) and the chopped spinach/basil. Simmer for 5 minutes or until the fish flakes easily and has fully changed its colour to white. Remove any fish bones if necessary.

- Just take the fish and tomatoes out and spoon some of the tomato sauce onto it.

If this is too thin you can add some ground arrowroot if you like. You only need to put the arrowroot into a jar with a bit of milk, shake it up to mix thoroughly, and stir it into the sauce (after removing the cod). That way the arrowroot completely dissolves with no lumps. Bring the sauce to the boil with the arrow root briefly, stirring. This will thicken it up.

Perhaps add a sprinkle of curry spice or more seasoning to the fish if you fancy.

LUNCH RECIPES

In this chapter I'm going to show you what lunch recipes I recommend -- plenty of soups, salads, quiches and a few hearty options to choose from.

SOUP RECIPES

Soups are easy to digest and super nourishing, so make sure you have them a lot. Here's a few good ones to get you started:

Bone Broth (GF, DF, SF)

Since Bone broth is one of the most effective and natural ways at healing your gut, it is a good idea to continue drinking it regularly.

The long cooking time makes the broth highly alkaline which encourages healing in your body and makes the food you eat afterwards more digestible.

Prep: 8 minutes   Cooking Time: 3-4 hours

Go to the broth recipe on page 17.

TIP: The next time you make Roast Chicken use the carcass straightaway to make Bone broth. Preferably with some meat and skin still attached. A slow cooker/ crock pot is very handy for this. But a saucepan works fine, too.

Chicken Soup (GF, DF)

Now we're talking chicken -- What has been used as cure and immune system boosting food in Eastern countries for centuries, can only be good for us, too, right ;-)

Prep: 5 minutes   **Cooking time: 20-30 minutes**

Makes 4 servings.

Ingredients:

- 1 chicken breast (cut into thin small strips)
- 1 leek
- 1/2 a big onion
- 2 chicken stock cubes in 1l (1 quart) or more water (or for an extra mineral boost: bone broth)
- Handful of cauliflower or broccoli florets
- Handful of frozen peas

Here's how you make it:

- Sauté the chicken in a little olive oil with salt, pepper and turmeric. Put aside.
- Chop and sautéthe onion and leek. Briefly add the broccoli, but don't fully cook.
- Bring the water to the boil, dissolve the chicken stock cubes and add this to the onions, leek and broccoli (or use bone broth for that).
- Add the chicken strips and peas, simmering for 20-30 minutes or until the chicken is cooked through (white in the center) and the veg is tender.

Cauliflower & Almond Soup (GF, DF, V)

This soup is as simple as it is creamy.

And the toasted almond flakes give it a sophisticated touch, which makes it a lovely starter to serve when you have guests.

Prep: 4 minutes   Cooking time: 25 minutes

Ingredients:

- 1 small cauliflower
- 2 big red onions finely chopped
- 1 big white onion finely chopped
- 1.5 stock cubes (4 tsp bouillon powder or broth)
- 2 handfuls of almonds freshly roasted

Here's how you make it:

- Bring 1.5 l (1.5 quarts, 6 cups) water to the boil and dissolve the stock cubes in it (or simply use broth.
- Chop the onions and wash and chop the cauliflower into medium sized chunks.
- Lightly fry the onions in a little olive oil with salt, pepper, turmeric (Kurkuma) and cayenne pepper until soft and golden. Add the cauliflower bits and toss in the onion mix for a couple of minutes. Then transfer the vegetables to a big pot with the hot stock.
- Simmer for 25 minutes.
- Lightly roast the flaked almonds in a small frying pan over a medium heat, careful not to burn them. Add half of them to the soup and set the rest aside.
- Blend the soup to a creamy consistency and sprinkle the rest of the almonds over it when serving.

Cavolo Nero (Kale) & Pork Soup (GF, DF)

This Soup is totally delicious! In every sense of the word. It is nourishing. It is simple to make. It looks good. And it even satisfies the demands of a hungry meat eater boyfriend ;-) Perfect!

And once blended, you're left with a filling thick soup that tastes absolutely gorgeous and contains health boosting ingredients to boot.

This soup is also a great alternative if you can't eat potatoes, because the canellini beans give it a potato-ey flavor. I made one version just with beans and one with beans and meat, both taste great. But meat has the added bonus of extra protein, making the dish more filling (without having to add more carbs like pasta, rice or quinoa).

Prep: 2 minutes   Cooking time: 25 minutes

Ingredients:

- 2-3 small to medium sized cavolo nero leaves (or savoy cabbage leaves)
- 1 l stock (I used chicken, but veg works fine, too – or bone broth for extra nourishment)
- 2 leeks
- Spices for seasoning (I used salt, pepper, cayenne, garlic and tumeric)
- Olive Oil for frying and marinating

Optional:
- 2-3 slices of roast pork (or roast chicken/ turkey).
- a dash of apple cider vinegar to tenderize and marinate the meat (if using)

Here's how you make it:

- If using meat you could marinate it in a little olive oil, spices and apple cider vinegar and set it aside.
- Chop the leeks and cavolo nero into bite size chunks.
- Then saute the leek in a little olive oil, salt & pepper until golden and soft.
- Bring 1 l stock to the boil. Add all the veg and simmer for about 20 minutes.
- Towards the end add the finely chopped roast meat if you like).
- Bring to the boil briefly and let it simmer for a few more minutes. Adjust the seasoning if necessary.
- Either serve as is or blend to make a thick creamy soup.

Creamy, hearty, YUM!

SALADS &
QUICK LIGHT BITES

Salads make a healthy lunch choice that you can even prepare the day before. The ones I'm about to show you are real classics and very filling. They make great lunch box choices, too.

Salad with Grilled Chicken (GF, DF, SF)

A light dish that gives you lots of energy.

Makes 2 servings

Prep: 5 minutes   Cooking time: 20 minutes

(can be cut down to 5 minutes if you prepare the chicken breast the day before and this is just to reheat it)

Ingredients:

- Small gem or romaine lettuce
- 1 chicken breast
- 4 ripe tomatoes
- Half a yellow bell pepper
- Third of a cucumber
- Olive oil and dash of apple cider vinegar
- Seasoning to taste (turmeric, cayenne, salt, black pepper)

Optional:

- Handful of sunflower seeds

Here's how you make it:

- Grill the chicken breast for ten minutes from both sides *(I marinated the chicken in the marinade from page 147 beforehand)*.
- Chop and mix all the salad ingredients, letting it sit in the salad sauce for a few minutes.
- Roast the sunflower seeds over a low heat in a frying pan.
- Cut the chicken breast in equal sized strips and layer over your salad in a bowl. Then sprinkle with the roasted sunflower seeds.

Note:
Keeps in the fridge for another day. Store the chicken pieces separately though.

Salad Niçoise - Salad with Tuna & Boiled Egg (Simple) (GF, DF)

Filling and you'll have leftovers for the next day, too - yay!

Prep: 4 minutes   Cooking time: 7 minutes

Ingredients

- Half a gem or romaine lettuce
- 2 tomatoes
- Half a red bell pepper
- Half a big tin of tuna
- 2 small eggs

Optional:

- Bunch of parsley or chives finely chopped
- For the salad sauce: sea salt, freshly ground black pepper, cayenne pepper, apple cider vinegar, olive oil

Here's how you make it:

- Chop the tomatoes into quarters or smaller. Slice the bell pepper into thin strips and the gem lettuce into chunks. Mix it in a big bowl with a dash of apple cider vinegar and 1 tbsp olive oil and about half a tsp of salt and pepper. Add the tuna flakes, stir and taste; if necessary adjust the seasoning.
- Meanwhile boil the eggs in boiling water for 7 minutes. Then rest them in cold water for a few seconds to stop the cooking process. Peel and either chop into small pieces that you mix in with the salad or just serve the halves on top of your salad with a bit of salt sprinkled on top.

Makes 2 portions, so you might want to store half of it in the fridge for the next day. Why not take this salad with you as a packed lunch?

Indian-Style Scrambled Eggs with Tomatoes & Prosciutto (GF, DF)

This is one of my absolute favorite Recipes - so tasty & quick to make!

It's an amalgamation of my Mum's German way of cooking Scrambled eggs and a recipe I've seen in a Curry cook book. It tastes awesome with freshly baked Sesame soda bread *(from Stage 3 of the Candida Diet onwards!)*

It also makes a perfect filling for whole meal pitta bread pockets with cheddar cheese. *Not that you could enjoy this just yet - this is a serving suggestion for your hungry family of non Candida sufferers ;-)*

Prep: 3-4 minutes   Cooking time: 10 minutes

Ingredients:

- 2 large eggs
- 5 cherry tomatoes (quartered)
- 1 small bunch chives, basil or spinach (finely chopped)
- 1 drizzle semi skimmed goats milk
- 1 pinch turmeric
- 1/2 teaspoon brown mustard seeds (don't use mustard if you don't have the seeds; tastes very different!)
- thin slices prosciutto (use lean organic bacon if you don't have prosciutto)
- pinch of salt & black pepper (use freshly ground black pepper & low sodium salt if you have and don't add salt until done, because you might find the prosciutto has already given it enough of a salty taste)

Here's how you make it:

- Heat the mustard seeds in a frying pan until they start to pop. Add turmeric, a bit of Olive oil and sauté the chopped tomatoes in it until soft. Meanwhile chop the prosciutto finely and sauté with the tomatoes. Break the eggs into a bowl and blend with a fork, adding a swig of milk. Add a pinch of pepper and turmeric when blending.

TIP: Blend the tomatoes and prosciutto in with the egg mixture briefly. That makes it easier to distribute when you put it back in the frying pan. Plus they don't get burned so quickly at the bottom of the pan. Now add half a teaspoon of butter to the frying pan.

- When the butter is frothy pour the egg mix back into the frying pan. Let it cover the entire base of the frying pan (6 inches/ 15cm or Wok works well for this).

- Sauté on a medium heat without stirring until it sets. Then s-l-o-w-l-y stir the egg mix with a wooden spoon or spatula until it softly folds and builds big swirly egg nests. Turn these over if you like your eggs lightly brown. And there you have your scrambled eggs with a twist. If necessary adjust the seasoning, and sprinkle the chives, basil or spinach on before serving. Serve with a big green salad with sesame, pumpkin & sunflower seeds, salt, pepper and olive oil. Best eaten for lunch.

NICE VARIATION: Instead of the chives you can add finely chopped basil or fresh spinach towards the end of cooking.

Sardines and Boiled Egg (GF, DF)

Can't get any quicker - this has got to be the fastest lunch option

Prep: 0   **Cooking time: 6-7 minutes**

Ingredients

- 1 tin of sardines, drained
- 1-2 soft boiled eggs (6 minutes - egg still soft in the center; 7 minutes hard)

Optional:

- a chunk of cucumber, small salad, steamed green beans or tomatoes
- Seasoning to taste

Grain free Pie Crust (Paleo & GF, DF)

This is so quick to make and good enough to nibble on it's own ;-)

The idea for using almond flour for anything other than a cake recipe was revolutionary for me (I believe I first saw it on the Elana's Pantry website and I have been playing with variations of her base recipe ever since).

Prep: 0-1 minute   Time to make: 8-10 minutes

SAVORY PIE CRUST:

Ingredients:

- 230g (2 cups) almond flour
- 2 heaped tbsp ground flax seeds with 8 tbsp water (or 2 eggs)
- 1 tsp low salt, garlic or sea salt
- 4 tbsp coconut oil

Optional:

- 1 tsp of Italian herbs (like oregano, thyme, basil)

Here's how you make it:

- Warm the oil and mix all the ingredients together in a food processor. Press half the dough into a well oiled or buttered 9-inch (23cm) pie form lined with parchment paper.
- Fill with the filling of your choice (see suggestions below for ideas) and bake for 10-14 minutes. Or blind bake the crust without a filling at 350F (177 C) Gas 4 for about 8-10 minutes until firm to the touch and the edges look golden.
- Shape the rest of the dough into a ball and freeze. Take it out the night before you want to use it again; once defrosted, roll it out between two sheets of floured greaseproof paper or simply press it into shape with your fingers into a buttered pie form and bake as usual.

3 Simple pie filling ideas (you can bake with the pie crust in one go)

- Any type of stir-fried, grilled or cooked vegetables, lightly seasoned works nicely!
- For instance: chicken & leek or as in the picture above tenderstem broccoli, leek and bacon stir-fried
- Tuna, onion & tomato filling (just saute chopped onion and tomato with tomato paste, olive oil salt, pepper, towards the end add garlic and some drained flakes of tinned tuna - simple)

Pie crust Trouble-shooting:
If the pie crust doesn't come out in one piece, break it up and use it as a crumble topping for hearty stews or wrap it in tin foil and munch as a snack.

One word of warning though: Go easy on the almonds. As tasty as they are, when eaten in big quantities they can cause you to feel lethargic, headachy or cause bloating and constipation. To be on the safe side drink a glass of water to help your body process the big amount of fibre, and you'll be fine.

More Healthy Choices

Broccoli, Leek & Bacon Quiche Pg. 36

Grain/ Egg Free Quiche Pg.37

Roast Chicken with Gravy Pg.39

Lamb/ Beef Bolognese Pg 40

Salmon & Greens Pg.41

Thai Green Curry Pg.42

Creamy Veg Soup Pg. 43

Grilled Tuna with Salsa Pg. 44

Cabbage Salmon Rolls Pg.46

Ratatouille Pg.38

Grilled Fish/ Chicken Pg.47

Coconutty Yogurt Pg.48

Oven Omelet (with veggies and/or bacon) (GF, DF with V option)

Much less chance of burning, than on the hob -- set & forget!

Prep: 3 minutes   **Time to make: 15-20 minutes**

For instance Broccoli & Tomato with a few slices of red Ramiro Pepper (and/ or Bacon):

Ingredients:

- 6-7 medium broccoli florets.
- half a red ramiro pepper (or bell pepper) sliced into thin rings
- 2-3 eggs
- sea salt and freshly ground black pepper to taste

Optional:

- 4 rashers of bacon

Here's how you make it:

- Steam the broccoli for 3-4 minutes and grill and chop the bacon if using.
- Then simple whisk 2-3 eggs with a little salt and black pepper, place the veggies and bacon on the pie crust or straight into a greased pie form and pour the eggs on top.
- Bake for 15 to 20 minutes at 350F (177 C) Gas 4 until solid in the center. Check toward the end of the baking time and cover with a lid or tin foil if edges are starting to darken.

Quiche (with Topping of Your Choice)
e.g. Leek, Tenderstem Broccoli & Bacon) (GF, can be V)

Prep: 5 minutes   **Time to make: 20-30 minutes**

Here's how you make a Quiche without a pie or pastry base:

- Like the Oven Omelet just mix in a few tbsp of yogurt or cottage cheese (and any other veg or meat filling) to the eggs before pouring over the filling. Add more salt and season ing if required.

- Bake at 350F (177 C) Gas 4 for around 20-30 minutes until a skewer inserted in the center comes out clean. Carefully separate the pie crust edges from the parchment paper with a knife. Lift the pie on the paper out of the pie form and let it cool on a wire rack. After 10 minutes carefully remove the paper with help of a knife.

Grain & Egg free Quiche (GF, DF, V)

This dish is quick to make, versatile & yummy!

A real life saver on those days when you need to re-balance your system (by not eating meat, fish, grains and eggs -- which are all highly acidic and can add to the aches and pains and sadness you might be experiencing in your healing).

Who says you can only enjoy Quiche with eggs? Here's a great allergy-friendly egg-free alternative. You can use any type of vegetables for this.

Tip: *Double the chickpea flour and broth amount, add a few tomatoes and a chopped bell pepper to the mix. , and bake 10 minutes longer. Then you'll have extra leftovers for freezing ;-)*

You don't need a pie crust to make this lovely quiche.

Prep: 5 minutes   Cooking time: 30-40 minutes

Ingredients

- 1/2 tsp sea or low salt & 1/2 tsp of black pepper
- 2 cups of broccoli (chopped) (150g = 2 handful)
- 2 cups of red onions (150g = 1 big onion)
- 1 1/4 cup (136g) chickpea flour(besan)
- 1 1/2 cup veggie stock (245ml boiling water with 1/2 stock cube or equal amount broth)
- 2 tbsp oil (coconut or olive oil)
- Sprinkle of garlic powder
- 1 tomato or a dash of tomato paste

Here's how you make it:

- Preheat the oven to 400F (200C and gas 6).
- Saute the onions with a little oil, salt and pepper until soft. Add the broccoli in small florets and sauté for about 8 minutes until golden and almost cooked.
- Then whisk the chickpea flour in the hot stock until dissolved until it forms a loose paste consistency, similar to pancake batter. Stir in the tomato paste and oil.
- Fill the vegetables into a greased oven proof dish (I used a round one, 9 inch). Spread the chickpea batter over the vegetables so they are evenly covered.
- Bake for 30-40 mins or until a skewer inserted in the center comes out clean.

Ratatouille with Coconut Rice (GF, DF, V)

Here's a lovely Mediterranean-style recipe for you to try.

Granted the cooked veggies and brown rice *do* contain some natural sugars. Feel free to serve the meal with fish to balance the carbs load of the dish.

Prep: 5 minutes   Cooking time: 35-40 minutes

Ingredients:

- 1 medium aubergine (thinly sliced & cubed)
- 2 small courgettes (sliced)
- 3 organic bell peppers (any color)
- 1 large red onion (coarsely chopped)
- 3 cloves garlic (peeled and crushed)
- salt & black pepper & turmeric
- olive oil
- 1 can organic tomatoes (make sure there's no citric acid in it - if you can't find one without use 4 ripe tomatoes instead)
- tomato paste (about half a tube)
- 1/2 cup or more; 60g brown rice or double the amount if making some for the next day ;-)
- 1 tablespoon coconut oil

Here's how you make it:

- Heat the mustard seeds in a frying pan until they start to pop. Add turmeric, a bit of Olive oil and fry the chopped tomatoes in it until soft. Cut the aubergines into 1cm thin slices and sauté them first as they need longest to soften.
- Then chop the rest of the vegetables into bite-size chunks; disregarding the core of the bell peppers. Ideally chop the bell peppers not too small as they disintegrate easily. Add all veg to the frying pan, stirring regularly. Get the garlic ready while the veg is cooking.
- Add the garlic after 10-15 minutes of cooking.
- Then add the tomatoes and tomato puree. Season well. Continue to cook without lid for 15 more minutes or until the bell peppers' skins are soft. It's ready when the liquid has reduced down to a creamy consistency.
- Season with salt & pepper. Bring 1 l of water to the boil. Add a pinch of salt. Wait until it's boiling again, then add the rice. Simmer the rice for 35-40 minutes until soft.   Stirring occasionally and making sure there is sufficient water in the pot. If necessary pour in more boiling water.
- Drain & add the coconut oil, stirring until it has melted and is distributed evenly. Serve with a green salad, some fresh spinach leaves or simply on its own.

NICE VARIATION:

As mentioned before, Ratatouille tastes great with steamed or grilled fish; which also makes the dish a bit more filling and even more Candida Diet friendly.

Roast Chicken with Red Onion Gravy (GF, DF)

Now here's one of my all time favorite recipes – a proper Chicken Roast – an absolute Classic!

Tip: Why not make it once a week and use your left-overs in a lovely curry, heart-warming soup or nourishing Bone broth ;-)

I recommend you buy the freshest AND biggest organic chicken you can get (even if you don't have a big family to feed or you're hard up) -- **freeze small portions of the cooked meat in ziplog bags. This comes in handy when you don't have mu**ch energy to cook, and the addition of meat makes soups, lentil & beans dishes more filling! It might initially cost more, but a whole chicken will keep you going for a long time; well worth it!

Prep: 5 minutes   **Cooking time: 1hr 20 minutes**

Ingredients:
- 1 medium organic chicken
- 1-2 medium red onions
- 1 small red bell pepper
- 2 medium carrots
- ground arrow root (for thickening the gravy)
- olive oil
- 2 cloves garlic
- salt & freshly ground black pepper & turmeric & cayenne pepper
- 1-2 stick celery

Here's how you roaast the chicken:

- Preheat your oven to 240 degrees c/ 475 f/ gas 9
- Wash the veg and chop them into big chunks. Peel the garlic and put it on a deep oiled roasting tray together with the veg.
- Drizzle the veg with olive oil. Then drizzle the oil over the chicken, too; rubbing salt & pepper (and turmeric & cayenne if using) onto its skin. You can also add fresh herbs like rosemary at this stage.
- Sit the chicken on top of the veg onto the roasting tray and put it in the oven. Turn the heat down to 200c/ 400f/ gas 6 and cook the chicken for 1hr and 20 minutes.
- Set a timer for 40 mins and check on the veg. If they look dry add water to the tray. Baste the chicken with olive oil and salt and pepper and let it cook for another 40 minutes. When cooked, take the chicken out and let it rest on the side wrapped in tin foil whilst you make the gravy.

Here's How You Make Awesome Gravy:

- Heat 1/2l (1/2 quart) of water and when boiling add 1 yeast free chicken stock cube (or use home-made stock if you have) and whisk this up. Put the tray over a high heat on the hob, add some ground arrow root and stir to thicken the gravy up. (If there is a lot of fat swimming on top of the veg tray you can remove some of it with a spoon before heating it up).

- Use a potato masher or fork to mash the vegetables into a pulp. I personally like to have some onion rings and veg bits still in there for a rustic taste and look. But you can blend this more or put it through a sieve if you prefer a smooth consistency.

Note: This makes a lot of gravy. For 1-2 people I'd recommend to use 0.5 l (0.5 quarts) of water and only one ½ stock cube or 2 tsp of stock powder (unless of course you want to eat the gravy the next day). You might need more water and a bit of veg if you're making this recipe with chicken joints rather than the whole chicken (works just as well though). Serve this dish with steamed broccoli or other greens of your choice.

Lamb or Beef Bolognese Stew (GF, DF)

Serve with Courgette/ Zucchini Noodles rather than pasta -- very tasty!

Prep: 5 minutes   Cooking time: 45 minutes

Basic Sauce:

Ingredients:

- 3 1/3 cups (450g) organic minced lamb; veggie alternative: red lentils
- 2 big white onions
- 1 tin of organic chopped tomatoes (preferably without citric acid)
- 1 tube of tomato paste (called puree in the UK)
- pinch of salt and garlic granules
- 2 garlic cloves, chopped finely

Optional Sauce Additions:
- pinch of ground fenugreek
- ½ tsp tandoori curry spice
- pinch of paprika
- 2 handfuls of fresh spinach

For the spice mix:
- 1 tsp of coriander seeds
- ½ tsp of cumin seeds
- ½ tsp of fennel seeds
- ½ tsp of dark mustard seeds
- salt, pepper

Here's how you make it:

- Chop & saute two big onions in olive oil until they are brown.
- Saute 450 g (3 1/3 cups) organic lamb (or beef) mince. Add a bit of apple cider vinegar to tenderize the meat.
- Briefly roast the seeds over a low heat, then grind them finely.
- Stir the spices into your bolognese sauce.
- Let it simmer for 25 minutes or longer. It does actually taste even nicer, the longer it cooks.Towards the end add some chopped spinach. Adjust the seasoning if needed.
- Serve with thin Zucchini (courgette) strips instead of pasta.

DINNER RECIPES

Whenever you want to lose weight (or give your body optimum conditions for healing) cook these healthy protein rich meals:

Steamed Salmon with Greens, Beans & Peas (GF, DF, SF with V option)

Super quick and one of my top healing meals by none, it's so anti-inflammatory!

I literally eat it whenever I feel a bit under the weather or want to lose some weight -- it works extremely well!

Prep: 4 minutes   Cooking time: 8-10 minutes

Ingredients:

- 1 medium slice of fresh salmon (or frozen)
- a few asparagus stalks (carefully remove all hard, stringy bits)
- 1 handful fine green beans or frozen broad beans (fava beans)
- a couple of broccoli florets
- 1 handful peas
- olive oil dressing (with salt, freshly ground pepper, cayenne pepper and fresh garlic or garlic granules and a pinch of turmeric)

Here's how you make it:
- Chop the vegetables and arrange them around the salmon in a steamer. Steam for 8-10 minutes; then add the peas.
- Meanwhile make the dressing which you can drizzle over the salmon and veg when done.

Notes:
- Make extra veggies, so you can reheat some the next day. Tastes especially lovely with pumpkin seed, sesame or flax oil, salt and pepper and some pumpkin and sun flower seeds!
- When using frozen fish, best take the fish out a few hours beforehand so it can defrost. That way it stays tender. Otherwise quickly heating from frozen tends to make the fish a bit chewy.

If you're just steaming the fish and no veg then you're probably done in under five mins - fish steams super fast. No prep. No fuss. If you like salmon this will be one of your staple dishes from now on.

VEGGIE/ VEGAN VARIATION:

Stir-fried white cabbage with butter or spring greens and red chilli & sesame oil work also beautifully... and from stage 3 onwards you can also have some sweet potato or potato with it for an extra vitamin, mineral and alkaliniy kick.

Thai Green Curry... delicious & mild! (GF, DF with V option)

This mild version of a Thai Green Curry is super quick to make and just tastes heavenly. One of my fav's!

Tastes great with shrimp/ king prawns, chicken or just veggies.

Prep: 3 minutes   Cooking time: 25-30 minutes

Ingredients:

- 400g (14 oz, 13/4 cups) shrimp/king prawns (best fresh but frozen are ok, too)
- 3 tablespoons olive oil
- 1 handful mangetouts (snow peas) or sugar snaps or green beans
- 1 small red pepper
- 1 large leek
- 1 clove garlic
- 1 teaspoon mild curry powder (Check the ingredients list that there's no yeast extract or acetic acid in it)
  half a teaspoon turmeric, salt & freshly ground black pepper

Optional:

- half a can coconut milk (pick a good one without citric acid - you'll really taste the difference!)
- 1 teaspoon fennel seeds
- half a teaspoon cumin seeds
- 150g rice pasta or brown rice

Here's how you make it:

- If you've decided to have coconut rice with it you need to set the brown rice cooking first as this takes the longest cooking time. Rice pasta needs less than half the cooking time ;-)
- Heat a wok (or big frying pan) up over a high heat and roast the seeds briefly before adding 2 table spoons of olive oil. If you'd rather make rice pasta then set them cooking in boiling water now with about 1/4 tsp of sea salt (if using).
- Chop the red pepper finely, the leek into big rings and the mangetouts in half. Then mix and sauté with the seeds until tender. Perhaps adding a little bit of water if it's too dry.
- In a separate frying pan quickly sauté the king prawns/ shrimp in a little olive oil with salt, pepper, tumeric, cayenne pepper and freshly chopped garlic (you could do this the night before if your time was limited; then you'd only need to make the rice and veggies sauce the next day). When crisp and lightly coated in spices add to the veg, stirring well. Pour the coconut milk over the curried veg and king prawns/ shrimp and let it simmer for 15 minutes.

Once you've tried this dish you'll be cooking it again and again, as it is very tasty and so quick to make.

VEGGIE VARIATION:

You can swap the shrimp/ king prawns for chicken or simply add more veg for a vegetarian variation if you like. Still tastes delicious!

Creamy Veg Soup with Crispy Turkey (GF, DF, V, with Paleo option)

This vegetable soup is one to remember!

Most Candida Diet recipes can leave you still feeling hungry. Not this one. It is full of goodness and a joy to eat for the entire family.

Prep: 6 minutes   Cooking time: 30 minutes

Ingredients:

- 1 red pepper
- 2 sticks of celery
- 1 small cauliflower
- 2 leeks
- 1 red onion
- 3 tablespoons olive oil
- salt and freshly ground black pepper, cayenne pepper and turmeric & freshly ground black pepper
- 2 yeast free chicken stock cubes/broth

Optional:

- 1-2 cloves of garlic
- 1 small carrot (from stage 3 of the diet onwards)
- 1 small potato (from stage 3 of the diet onwards)
- 3 rashers of bacon (or a handful of roasted seeds e.g. sunflower, sesame & pumpkin)
- 400g (14oz) skinless diced turkey meat (later on during the diet feta also works nicely)

Here's how you make it:

- Peel the onion, (carrot and potato) and roughly chop all the vegetables that you want to use. Heat a large pan and add 2 tablespoons of olive oil. Add a bit of salt, pepper, cayenne and turmeric according to your taste and sauté the onion and red pepper in it until they are soft. Add the rest of the vegetables and cook for about 10 minutes with the lid askew, stirring frequently.

- Now is a good time to add the finely chopped garlic if using. Bring 1.8 l (7.8 cups; 1.6 quarts) of water to the boil in a big saucepan. Add the stock cubes/ broth and stir until they are dissolved.

- Add the vegetables; turning the heat down again so they are cooking on a low-medium heat. Leave them to simmer for 20 minutes until they are soft. Then mash with a smoothie maker, hand blender or liquidizer. I tend to prepare the turkey fresh towards the end of the cooking time of the soup. Then the strips are nice and hot. But you can just as easily prepare the turkey meat now and reheat before serving the soup.

- All you do is sauté them briefly with the spices in a little olive oil until they are slightly crisp and brown. When you filled your serving bowl with soup you can scatter a few turkey strips on top of your soup or you serve them separately. You can also add the fried turkey strips to the soup before blending. This makes the soup even thicker and creamier which is lovely. I'd still keep a few to decorate your soup with ;-) Alternatively srinkle the roasted seeds on the top. Additionally you can put a few rashers of lean un-smoked organic bacon under the grill.

Grilled Tuna Steak with Tomato Salsa (GF, DF)

This dish is so good for you that you should enjoy it regularly. Especially when you're feeling a bit under the weather.

You can swap the tuna for other oily fish if you like. Salmon is great for instance; or serve it with a red pepper & cucumber salsa like here on the photo.

Prep: 3 minutes   Cooking time: 4-6 minutes

Ingredients:

- Extra Virgin Olive Oil
- Salt & freshly ground pepper, cayenne pepper and turmeric
- Drizzle of freshly squeezed lemon juice
- A small garlic clove
- 1 fresh tuna steak
- 2 handfuls fine green beans
- 2 handfuls cherry tomatoes
- A few basil leaves

Here's how you make it:

For the Fine Green Beans & Tomato Salsa:

- Wash and prepare the fine green beans and steam them for 20 minutes or until tender. Chop the cherry tomatoes and lightly fry them in a little olive oil with a dash of spice. Meanwhile finely chop the garlic and basil. Add them to the tomatoes once they are soft and smell sweet.

For the Grilled Tuna Steak:

The tuna virtually does not need any cooking - it's so quick to make.

- You can either put it under the grill for a few minutes each side. Or you can zap it in a griddled frying pan briefly from both sides. It generally does not take longer than 2-3 minutes each side.

Be careful not to overdo it. When you leave it in too long it gets an unpleasant rubbery consistency.

We are aiming for lightly brown on the outside and lightly pink or just white on the inside. Then it's lovely succulent and tender. And with a drizzle of fresh lemon juice it's even easier to digest.

This makes it one of the very few allergy-friendly & quick to cook healthy dinner recipes. Eat grilled tuna steak (or other fish) 2-3 times a week and you are doing your body a massive favor, because this dish has lots of anti-inflammatory properties and is fairly easy to digest.

Once turned over and crisp on both sides you can chop it up and mix it in with your soup. My personal favorite is to sprinkle the bacon on top of the soup when you have filled your serving bowl.

This makes enough for 2 people for 2 meals. Serve it with a green salad and any of the toppings listed above and you might even have another portion left over for freezing :)

VEGAN TOPPING:

Instead of the Turkey/ bacon roast some Sunflower, Pumpkin or Sesame seeds with a little spice (I used sea salt, black pepper, kurkuma/turmeric and a pinch of cayenne) and add this as a topping before serving. Desiccated coconut works well, too. A nice contrast to the velvety texture of the soup.

VEGETARIAN TOPPING (FROM STAGE 3 ONWARDS)

Crumble some feta over the soup before serving. With or without roasted seeds a real delight.

Note:

This soup freezes well, so why not straight away make double the amount?!

Cabbage Rolls with Salmon (GF, DF)

Delicious with bone broth or home made gravy, and ridiculously good for you :-)

Prep: 1 minute   Cooking time: 1 minute

Ingredients:

- 4 big cabbage leaves plus 6 smaller ones or more as a side (I used Savoy)
- 2 pieces of salmon
- leftover gravy or bone broth
- Metal or wooden skewers if you have (can be made without)

Here's how you make it:

- Steam the fish for 15-20 minutes until the insides go from pink to whitish/ pink. That's when it flakes off easily and tastes succulent.   Any longer and it can get chewy. It's easiest in a steamer. But if you haven't got one you can sit the fish in a colander inside a pot with bubbling hot water.

- Meanwhile remove the outer cabbage leaves or the next ones that look good. Wash them and toss in a big pot with lightly salted cooking water. Blanch for 5-10 minutes to soften. They should be cooked but not so much that they lose color and get all floppy.

- Take leaves out and dry between kitchen towels. Put a third or half of a piece of salmon in the center of a cabbage leaf. Sprinkle salt and freshly ground pepper on top.

- Flip the bottom of the cabbage leaf (the part with the stem) upwards and pin it with one hand on top of the salmon (just like nappy changing really ;-). Then fold the left cabbage leaf side and the right one to meet on top of the salmon where you are holding it down.

- Then fold the top of the leaf down, too. Now you have a roll or parcel shape.

- You can either fix the salmon cabbage roll with a metal skewer on both sides to hold the filling in.

- Or you turn the parcel round (with the loose folded sides towards the work surface) and hope that the weight will hold it in place. You might have to fold it again with less filling to make it easier to retain the shape.

- This is great use for any leftover gravy from making Roast Chicken. Heat the gravy up in a big pot and once it's hot pour it over the cabbage rolls. Alternatively, if the rolls are firmly tucked together you could sit the rolls in the gravy (or bone broth, delicious!) and simmer for a bit.

- Serve two parcels with additional cabbage per person. From Stage 3 onwards you can serve the salmon rolls with cooked potatoes or brown rice.

QUICK FOOD PREP TIPS

Steam Fish and Vegetables

Prep: 0   **Cooking time: 3-6 minutes**

So quick & it brings out the flavor nicely and generally keeps the nutritional value of your food more intact than cooked any other way!

Grilled Chicken/ Grilled Fish with Vegetables

Prep: 0   Cooking time: 10-20 minutes

5 minutes each side (cut into strips); 10 minutes each side (whole chicken breast)

Grilling is a quick way to prepare fish or meat, or even vegetables. I have only recently started doing this because before then I always perceived it as this complicated long process involving you to constantly check on the food to make sure it's not burning. Well, it's not like that.

Here's how I do it:

I baste the fish or meat in this marinade: 1 dash of apple cider vinegar, about 1 tbsp of olive oil and season it from both sides with sea salt, black pepper, cayenne pepper, turmeric, a sprinkle of garlic granules and paprika.

Then I place it on a rack covered with tin foil under the grill with medium heat. **Chicken breast generally takes 10 minutes** from each side, less if you cut it into strips. **Fish only takes about 6 minutes** from each side, sometimes even less if it's thin.

I let it sit on the side for a moment. Before serving I squeeze the juice of a slice of lemon over the fish. Serve with steamed/ cooked or stir fried veggies. If you're grilling the veggies as well you might have to remove the skin afterwards, as veg tends to char when grilled.

Baked Chicken/ Fish/ Veggies Parcels in the Oven
Prep: 1 minute   Cooking time: 30 minutes

If you want to get on with other stuff while the food is cooking, then baking or slow cooking is your best option. Just prepare the fish/ meat/ veggies with the marinade as before. But instead of putting them under the grill place them in the center of a piece of tinfoil that is big enough to wrap around the food, then fold all corners up towards the center creating little food parcels.

Sitting the marinaded fish on a bed of seasoned green beans inside the parcel for instance works beautifully. With fish I recommend putting a bunch of chopped parsley in the parcel. With chicken or vegetables some herbs you might have on hand like thyme, basil or rosemary.

Try using a slow cooker/ crock pot

Prepares your food 2 to 8 hrs in advance. Set it going in the morning for dinner or before going to bed to have it cooking over night. Awesome for tenderizing meat & cooking hearty vegetable- beans or lentil stews.

DESSERTS

Keep desserts to a minimum these next two weeks.
You'll soon be able to eat rich puddings again -- hang in there!

Yogurt with Coconut, Seeds with Nuts Sprinkled on Top (GF, egg free, can be nut free)

Hey, this really is sugar free. It DOES take some getting used to!

You'll inevitably miss the sweetness you're accustomed to from your usual off-the-shelf yogurts. But be good -- you'll soon be able to add sweetener to your desserts again. At least this one is *quick and filling!*

Prep: 1 minute   Cooking time: 0

Ingredients

- 2-4 heaped tbsp of plain probiotic yogurt (sheep is best if you can get hold of it, tastes milder and creamier than goat's yogurt, a bit more like Greek yogurt)
- dash of Cinnamon
- 1 handful of sunflower seeds (preferably pre-soaked over night)

Optional:
- 2 tbsp desiccated coconut (unsweetened & un-sulfured)
- a few nuts or almonds (preferably soaked overnight)

Here's how you make it:

- Fill the yogurt in a small bowl. Mix the coconut in and sprinkle the sunflower seeds on top with a dash of cinnamon.

Granted, if you are used to sweet conventional fruit yogurts then this will taste horrible at first. I remember that I couldn't stand plain yogurt and used to put honey in it to make it palatable. Unfortunately honey is lagged with sugar, so we cannot use it here. But what we can do is make the texture more interesting, adding a nice nutty crunch that will keep you full for longer.

I don't recommend adding sweetener because this will give you a taste for more sweet foods (even if you use stevia).

Fancy a Snack?

Chia Pudding
Pg.50

Crunchy Ricemilk Snack
Pg.51

Almond Butter Dough Balls
Pg.52

Coconut Pancakes
Pg.53

Spicy Chickpeas
Pg.54

Fried Egg Veg Snack
Pg.54

Hummus with Celery Sticks
Pg.54

Tuna Lettuce Snack
Pg.55

Sesame Kale Snack
Pg.55

Almond Butter
Pg.51

Carob Choc Alternative
Pg.51

Natural Yogurt
Pg.48

Chia Coconut Pudding (GF, DF, V)

Serve with whipped chilled coconut cream for a festive treat or chill in the fridge overnight for a super quick breakfast on-the-go.

Makes 2

Prep: 1 minute   Cooking time: 0

Ingredients:

- 8 tbsp chia seeds (1/3 cup)
- 1 cup rice milk
- 1 tbsp coconut cream (or use coconut milk instead of the rice milk and add 1-2 drops of vanilla stevia)

Optional:

- 1 tsp vanilla paste (or the inside scraped from 1/3 fresh vanilla bean)
- 4 tbsp desiccated coconut

Here's how you make it:

- Dissolve the coconut cream by stirring it in a small bowl with just enough boiling water to loosen it up.
- Then whisk the chia seeds in with with the rice milk and vanilla and coconut if using.
- Add a little more liquid if it looks too dry - the chia seeds will baloon to four times their dry size.
- Let it sit for 15 minutes to give the chia seeds time to soak up the liquid.

When and How Often Should You Indulge in Your Candida Diet Desserts?

Desserts are an integral part in family meals and happy meals full stop. Just because you are following a sugar free diet does not mean that you cannot have desserts.

- You just have to be a little bit more select about what you indulge in and when.
- What you don't want is overburden your system with rich & sweet foods that are likely to trigger food sensitivity or other symptoms.

Hence my suggestion for you would be to stick **to as little sweetener as possible** while you are still following the diet. Gradually, as you get better, you can then add sweeteners back into your diet (occasionally).

My advice in general would be to **have mid morning or mid afternoon snacks rather than desserts**. If you feel you cannot skip desserts then **get into the habit of waiting at least 30 minutes after a meal before eating your dessert**.

Happiness is key to your recovery. So enjoy and do things that make you happy :)

HEALTHY SNACKS

I couldn't let you follow a strict diet
without giving you some snack suggestions, right?!

Try and also have the healthy snacks from the previous chapter as often as possible though (avocados, cucumber slices, green juice/ smoothie -- page 14)

Unfortunately chocolate is off the books for the near future. But if you can't go without a sweet fix, you could occasionally snack on a Carob bar or make your own snack from quality cocoa, stevia and coconut oil. Do that only as a last resort though. I'm going to show you healthier options that can help you through this without making your symptoms worse. You could also have the occasional spoon full of almond butter alongside a glass of water or resort to one of the snacks below to tide you over...

Crunchy Rice Milk Snack (GF, DF, V)

Just hits that sweet spot, when you're cravings get the better of you...

Prep: 1 minute   Cooking time: 0

Ingredients:

- 2-4 tablespoons of sunflower seeds (preferably soaked in water and a dash of apple cider vinegar over night)
- 1/4 cup rice milk (115ml)
- 2 tbsp unsweetened and unsulfured desiccated coconut
- 1 tbsp flax oil
- 1/4 tsp cinnamon

This is one of my own candida snacks creations (she said proudly, the photo doesn't do it justice by the way) Sweet and exotic – a real alternative to porridge and puddings.

Here's how you make it:

Just add the rice milk to the sunflower seeds and coconut. Then prinkle with cinnamon – Yum!

Almond Butter Dough Balls (GF, DF, V)

As a special treat at the weekend. Chewy and sweet -- they'll be gone in a blink ;-)

Makes: 6 small balls (about 0.80 inch/ 2cm in diameter); just enough for one person really. You might have to triple or quadruple the amounts if you want some for your family as well.

Prep: 4 minutes   Cooking time: 0

Ingredients:

- 1/4 cup (20g) shredded unsweetened un-sulfured desiccated coconut; plus 1 tbsp for dusting.
- 1/2 cup (46g) unsweetened almond butter (ideally from blanched almonds tastes smoother and sweeter)
- 1/4 cup (30g) coconut flour
- about 4 tbsp of rice, unsweetened almond or coconut milk to mix (during the Candida elimination diet add 1-2 drops of Vanilla stevia sweetener if you're using almond milk/coconut milk as rice milk is naturally sweeter; once Candida levels are under control 1tbsp of maple syrup or raw honey would add just the right amount of sweetness)

Optional: 1tbsp of coconut oil (for an additional Candida fighting kick)

Here's how you make it:

- Mix all the ingredients in a food processor or by hand. The dough should be soft but not so sticky that it isn't pliable. If too sticky add more coconut flour or desiccated coconut. If too crumbly a little more melted coconut butter or more dairy free milk would do the trick.
- Form the dough into small bite size balls with your hands or a small cookie scoop if you have (you can also use a table spoon and use about 1tbsp worth of dough to form each mini dough ball.)
- Roll the dough balls in the rest coconut until evenly covered.
- Chill on a plate or small tray in the fridge for 30 minutes or longer (or eat straight away!) I guess you could even freeze them to have them on hand.

TIP: Try to eat no more than 2 dough balls in one sitting and drink a big glass of water with it to help your body digest the large amount of fibre.

Even Quicker Almond Butter Dough Ball Version

Prep: 1 minute   Cooking time: 0

For a quick sweet-fix roll 1 tsp of almond buttter (with 1-2 drops of Vanilla Stevia/ maple syrup if you have a sweet tooth!) in 1 tsp of coconut flour in a medium sized ball until all sides are dusted and not sticky any more. Alternatively you could roll it in 1tsp of desiccated coconut, or mix 1tsp of coconut milk (scoop only the creamy solid part out) in with your almond butter before rolling in the Coconut flour or desiccated Coconut, yum! I like all three! The coconut flour version reminds me of marzipan potatoes which I was a huge fan of as a kid, so that's a winner. Desiccated coconut is always good, adds a little crunch, whereas the coconut milk variation adds moisture and isn't quite as dense which also has it's plus points. Let's face it -- it's virtually impossible to eat just one snack ball... So you might as well make three different ones to compare (you can always use the leftover coconut milk in a smoothie or stir-fry.

Coconut Pancakes (GF, DF, V option)

Yummy little things --They remind me of "Poor man's omelet" (sweet fried bread) my mum used to make.

Makes 8 mini fluffy pancakes.

Prep: 2 minutes   Cooking time: around 10 minutes

Ingredients:

- 2 eggs (at room temperature; cold eggs stunt the rising of the batter)
- 1/2 cup (118ml) coconut milk (or goats milk)
- 1/4 cup (27g) coconut flour
- 1 tsp vanilla paste
- 1/2 tsp baking soda
- 1/4 tsp sea salt
- Coconut oil for sautéing

Optional:
- 1 sachet of stevia with erythriol (less if it's pure Stevia or 2-4 drops of liquid stevia)
- 1 tbsp of ground flax seeds if the batter is too runny (also helps to mask the egg taste with a more traditional pancakey taste)

Here's how you make it:

- Heat a frying pan and melt half a teaspoon's worth of coconut butter onto it.
- Whisk the ingredients together and ladle the pancake batter into the frying pan. Make 2-3 small ones at a time, around 2 inch diameter (smaller than the inside of your hand) on a medium heat. Careful not to burn or tear them apart (they are more fragile then regular pancakes).
- When the top looks solid turn them with help of a spatula. Then sauté on that side for a couple more minutes or until both sides are golden and crisp.
- Cool on a wire rack and eat hot or cold. Can also be frozen.

Super Quick Spicy Chickpeas (Garbanzo Beans) (GF, DF, V)

Makes 3 snack portions

Prep: 0   Cooking time: 1 minute

This dish is a firm favorite with my readers. Quite rightly so. It's super quick, tasty, and it stops any cravings in their tracks.

Here's how you make it:

- Empty a tin of rinsed Chickpeas (Garbanzo beans) into a sauce pan and heat in a little olive oil.
- Season with salt, pepper, a pinch of turmeric/ kurkuma and some garlic granules.

Fried Egg Snack (GF, DF)

This rustic treat is so filling, you can have it for lunch if you wanted to.

But you can just as well whip it up as a snack in between meals or prepare the day before. Take it out of the fridge and briefly zap it under the grill.

Prep: 1 minute   Cooking time: 5 minutes

Ingredients:

- 1 leek
- 3 eggs

Here's how you make it:

Sauté 1 chopped leek with 3 eggs and a bit of seasoning. Turn it over once and serve on a bed of lettuce leaves.

Makes 2 servings.

Veggy Sticks with Organic Hummus (GF, DF, V)

Fantastic healthy snack.

In the next chapter I'll show you how to make hummus yourself (page 147) – it's easy.

The best veggies for this are celery sticks due to their non existent sugar content and colon cleansing properties (I'm afraid you'll have to get over the taste for now!).

Tuna Snack with Gem Lettuce (GF, DF)

Here's another quick carb free snack for you.

Prep: 1 minute   Cooking time: 0

Ingredients:

- small tin of tuna (or use between 1/3 to 1/2 of a big one) or equal amount of cooked turkey minced meat
- 2-3 lettuce leaves (I used a few more as they were ssmall gem lettuce leaves)

Here's how you make it:

- Drain the juices and serve the tuna/ cooked meat on a bed of gem lettuce with a bit of freshly ground pepper and a sprinkle of salt.

Sesame, Kale and Coconut Stir-fry (GF, DF, V)

Great craving buster snack!

Prep: 2 minutes   Cooking time: 10-20 minutes

Ingredients:

- 4 handful of kale
- 2-3 tbsp Coconut or sesame oil
- Sale, pepper, turmeric, pinch of cayenne pepper

Optional:
- handful of desiccated coconut or sesame seeds
- some creamed coconut dissolved in hot water to make it creamier and more coconutty

Here's how you make it:

- Lightly sauté four handful of kale in a little coconut oil, sea salt, black pepper, chilli and tumeric (Kurkuma). You might need a little water so the kale doesn't burn. (You can half the cooking time by steaming the kale for a few minutes before sautéing).

- When the kale is soft and is starting to wilt sprinkle sesame seeds on top and stir, coating the kale with the seeds from all sides. Drizzle a little sesame oil over it or add a bit more coconut oil, and serve as snack or as a side. Put half of it aside for the next day.

Top Tip:

- You can also speed up the overall cooking time and make it easier to digest by steaming the kale beforehand or by marinating it finely chopped and tossed in sea salt and a dash of apple cider vinegar. Also makes a fantastic addition to soups and stews with a slice of crusty toasted bread or pancakes, yum!

The Alternative: Eat a Spoonful of Unsweetened Smooth Almond Butter (if eaten in moderation -- almonds are equally as hard to digest as nuts)

Deliciously sweet, so you feel like you're eating something naughty. But without the unwanted side effects. Almonds are great for wound and overall healing because they are rich in minerals and one of the few alkalizing foods.

It's easy to make your own by the way - I'll share my Cinnamon almond butter recipe with you in the next chapter. Remember the lighter the snack the better. So have **cucumbers and avocados** as often as you can. You want to give your immune system the best chance of recuperating before you relax your diet, right?!

So what about a thick coconutty Green Smoothie? Go to the recipe on page 28.

RECAP OF STAGE 2

Well done - you've drastically reduced your carbs and sugar intake! This is doing your health and immune system the world of good.

Your digestive system is getting a chance to recover from any grain sensitivities you might have developed from years of eating lots of wheat and processed foods. You have discovered a few tasty healthy snacks that help keep your cravings at bay.

Not to forget you most likely lost a few unwanted pounds, too. If you weren't able to stick to the diet completely due to work or other commitments, don't worry. We're just getting started.

And if you did follow the diet to a t, then I bet you can't wait to take a look at the carbs dishes you are allowed to have now. Oatmeal porridge, bread… let's check them out :)
But first let's take a look at what drinks options you got:

DRINKS (FOR ALL STAGES)

Water -- I recommend you drink **good quality filtered water**. Lot's of it! It's important to **alkalize your system** to aid recovery and also to feel good.

Instead of drinking coke, soda pop or alcoholic drinks have a **glass of water with a slice of lemon or some lemon juice**. It also aids digestion which is good.

Natural apple cider vinegar -- I swear by **apple cider vinegar**, it's so good.

I have a glass with 2 tsp of it next to my bed - it's the first thing I drink in the morning and again whenever I eat something very rich or meaty. Even my mum swears by it; she says it stopped her arthritis and made her more bendy. Same with taking flax oil every day, it's so good for your skin and joints.

Ginger tea -- I have swapped my morning coffee for freshly brewed ginger tea.

Takes only twenty minutes to brew and I make enough for half a week, so I only need to reheat it in the mornings. One of the best investments in your health you can make. Boosts your metabolism, combats nausea and colds and simply makes you more active (don't drink it past lunch time though, can keep you awake). Peel and finely chop a thumb size of fresh ginger root and simmer in boiling water for 20 minutes in one liter of water (dilute with more water before serving if too strong).

Chicoree coffee substitute - I didn't go straight from coffee to ginger tea. For quite some time a was drinking **green tea** and loved it, and I also went through a phase of drinking **hot water** in the morning. You just have to do what feels right for you. If you can't let go of coffee try to add some chicoree coffee to it at least, because it has an alkalizing balancing effect on the otherwise completely acidic coffee.

A few **loose herbal teas** should also be in your repertoire in my opinion. You can prevent and treat illnesses with it. I've been using certain teas **as home remedies** for several years now, and have had an amazing success with it.

Nettle tea -- *to cleanse and rejuvenate (has a really milk sweet flavour - the opposite of what you'd expect)*

Mullein tea -- *absorbs excess mucous when you have sniffles or eaten too acidic.*

Dandelion tea -- *aids digestion.*

Chamomile -- *to relax in the evening, bring inflammation down, and fall asleep quickly.*

Passionflower tea -- *if you wake up at night and have trouble going back to sleep (makes you dream vividly!)*

Uva Ursi tea -- *cleanses the urinary tract thereby preventing and curing bladder infections and also alleviating constipation.*

Hundred times better than the bitter black tea brew that most people drink, and you almost have to put sugar and milk in to make it taste alright. I'm not totally against it, but black tea does disrupt the micro-balance in your gut, so at least for long-term Candida sufferers it's best to swap to mild herbal alternatives to re-build your immune system.

Now if you're new to the world of herbal teas perhaps just go for a nice mint tea to begin with. But I do recommend trying one of the other herbal teas at some time. Drinking tea makes for such a pleasant calming ritual that can only benefit your wellbeing :)

Needless to say I don't advocate alcohol during this diet. When you meet friends and family away from home **order sparkling water with a slice of lemon or mint/ chamomile tea or if it's at someone's place bring a coffee substitute.**

Yannoh for instance tastes delicious and Barley cup isn't too bad either (not sure whether you can get those where you live though. See what you can get where you are that is alkalizing/ contains Chicoree but no sugar or artificial aroma. Have hot rice or almond milk with it, and you've almost got a latte ;-) When out with friends and when you're in Stage 4 you could occasionally have a **decaf latte**, if you couldn't resist the coffee shop charm. It's not ideal because of the milk sugars, but it's ok every once in a while. Don't drink fruit juices (not even freshly squeezed - unless of course you don't have a yeast imbalance, then fruit is absolutely fine). Add protein powder to your smoothies to make them more filling (hemp protein powder has the best nutritional benefits).

SAUCES & SPREADS

Hummus and Veggie Sticks (GF, DF, V)

Of all the glutenfree snacks I know this one is probably the most filling: Hummus

Prep: 0   **Time to make: 1 minute!**

Homemade or bought – organic hummus is always a fantastic addition to your diet. Eaten with celery sticks it also has a super positive effect on your digestion.

Cinnamon & Almond Butter Spread (GF, DF, V)

This is heaven -- creamy, buttery, healthy, home made… heaven!

Prep: 0   **Time to make: 1 minute**

Ingredients
- 1 cup (100g) blanched almonds
- 4 tbsp milk of your choice (for instance rice milk or almond milk)
- 1 tsp cinnamon, 1 tbsp flax oil
- Vanilla stevia to taste (I suggest no more than 1-2 drops of vanilla stevia)

Tastes great spread thickly on a freshly toasted slice of homemade bread.

Here's how you make it:

- Grind the almonds to a fine powder in a blender or coffee grinder.
- Add 4 tablespoons of rice or almond milk, 1 tablespoon flax oil and the cinnamon.
- Use a small whisk to combine all the ingredients to a buttery spread.

Congratulations! You've made it through the first part of the diet.

This is where the fun bit starts: You can start to re-introduce carbs back into your diet!

Pancakes, bread, cereal -- the works!

You can find the next next book in this series on Amazon. It's called Sugar Free & Easy Candida Diet Recipes (Stage3 and beyond), and it's full of easy recipes I think you'll love.

And if you've spotted any typos or incorrect measurements, descriptions or I missed something in one of the recipes then please let me know. This is my first ever recipes book. Chances are there'll be something I can improve.

Make sure you're on my email list to **Claim Your FREE Meal Plan, Resources List (and Secret Bonus ;-)-- go to candidadietplan.com/4weekly-meal-plans/** -- And get my latest recipes, health tips and updates emailed to you for free.

I'm also sharing tasty recipes from other blogs that caught my eye over on Facebook at https://www.facebook.com/CandidaDietPlan

and on Pinterest at http://www.pinterest.com/sandraboehner/

If you're on twitter, I'd love you to tweet me that you read my book @candidadiettips :)

You are taking your health into your own hands - *you're awesome*! Let's connect!

If you found my recipes collection useful, please go to the book on Amazon and "leave a review", that would help me in a big way.

WEEKLY MENU PLAN – STAGE 2 (STRICT PROTEIN DIET) - WEEK 1

Menu	Monday	Tuesday	Wednesday	Thursday	Friday	Saturday	Sunday
Breakfast	Coconut Rice	Pepper & Leek Omelette	Cod with Cherry toms	Coconut Rice	Pepper & Leek Omelette	Cod with Cherry Toms	Coconut Rice
Snack	Red Pepper & Cucumber Slices	Hummus & Celery	Green Juice	Green Juice	Spicy Chickpeas	Avocado	Slice of oven omelet
Lunch	Chicken Soup	Ratatouille with Coconut Rice	Bone Broth Indian-style Scrambled Eggs	Creamy Soup with Turkey	Creamy Soup with Turkey	Oven Omelet with Bacon, Leek & Peppers	Bone Broth Roast Chicken & Veg
Snack	Hummus & Celery	Veg with Flax oil, salt &pepper	Avocado	Spicy Chickpeas	Coconut Rice	Veg with Flax oil, salt &pepper	Avocado
Dinner	Salmon & Veg	Chicken Soup	Veggie Stir-Fry	Grilled Tuna	Thai Green Curry	Thai Green Curry	Salmon & Veg

WEEKLY MENU PLAN – STAGE 2 (STRICT PROTEIN DIET) - WEEK 2

Menu	Monday	Tuesday	Wednesday	Thursday	Friday	Saturday	Sunday
Breakfast	Coconut Rice	Green Pepper Omelette	Cod with Cherry toms	Coconut Rice	Leek Omelette	Cod with Cherry Toms	Kedgeree (fish, brown rice, egg)
Snack	Hummus & celery	Veg with Flax oil, salt &pepper	Crunchy Rice milk snack	Creamy Calmer Smoothie	Kale & Sesame/ coconut stir-fry	Coconut Pancakes	Almond Butter Dough Balls
Lunch	Bone Broth	Salad with Tuna & Boiled Egg	Bone Broth	Courgette & Pepper Quiche	Salad with grilled Turkey or Chicken Strips	Bone Broth	Bone Broth
	Cauliflower & Almond Soup		Indian-style Scrambled Eggs			Quiche with Broccoli, Bacon and Toms	Über-delicious Stir Fry
Snack/ dessert	Avocado	Probiotic Yogurt with ground seeds & cinnamon	Hummus & celery	Avocado	Veg with Flax oil, salt &pepper	Spicy Chickpeas	Chia Pudding
Dinner	Chicken Curry with veg	Cabbage Rolls with Salmon	Creamy Green Detox Soup with Coconut	Salmon & Green Veg	Grilled Tuna with tomato salsa	Über-delicious Stir Fry	Roast Chicken & Veg

General Online Retailers/ Stores where you can find Good Organic Foods:

Actually you can find the essentials pretty much in any grocery store if you look in their organic/health food aisle. Also keep an eye out for dedicated organic foods stores and farmers markets in your area. You can also get most things online at Amazon **(http://candidadietplan.com/candida-diet-plan-shop/)**. If you repeatedly order the same products you can "Subscribe to a regular delivery once a month or every 3-6 months" and **save up to 15%** -- quite useful for groceries and household products or bulk buying grains or superfoods – I use this for my chlorella and millet deliveries for instance.

You'll definitely be able to stock up on things like coconut oil, rice milk and often times speciality flours and seeds for instance in the stores mentioned below (sorted by country) -- they all have a good selection of organic foods and health food items:

U.S.:

- Whole Foods (wholefoodsmarket.com)
- Trader Joe's (traderjoes.com)
- Sam' Club (samsclub.com)
- WinCo (wincofoods.com) bulk buys
- Costco (costco.com) wholesale membership chain with a great selection on organic foods
- WalMart (walmart.com)
- Vitacost (vitacost.com) is another online store with great deals on supplements and organic foods.
- Nuts fresh from the farm at Superior Nut Company online (superiornut.com)

Outside of the U.S.:

If you don't live in the US you can get the essentials at Iherb (iherb.com) -- they ship worldwide.

Canada:

- Well.ca – big selection of nuts, seeds, bean flour, coconut flour
- Grain Process Enterprises – flours, seeds and nuts delivery in the Toronto area
- Gluten-free-grocery.com – as the name suggests gluten free flours, certified gluten free oats and other baking ingredients

Australia:

- Iherb.com or the nearest health food store in your town
- allergy train, organics Australia (allergytrain.com.au)
- organic buyers group (organicbuyersgroup.com.au) -- heaps of superfoods cheap!

Germany: In Germany you can get most organic foods at bigger supermarkets like "Marktkauf" and "Real" and special dietary items at your local "Bioladen" or "Reformhaus" or online.

Great Britain:

This is a list of reputable brands and suppliers of organic foods and kitchen essentials I use myself:

HERE'S WHAT I BUY AT MY LOCAL HEALTH FOOD SHOP (ARCHIE BROWN IN TRURO; CORNWALL, UK):

- Coconut oil -- Biona Organic
- Gluten free flour -- I occasionally buy Bob's Redmill gluten free flour mix and then use half of that and half of the cheaper supermarket variety below.
- Coconut Milk – Biona Organic (without E numbers or thickener)
- Swiss Vegetable Vegan Bouillon Powder Reduced Salt -- Marigold
- Xylitol Sweetener – XyloBrit
- Tinned Tomatoes without citric acid -- or local health food shop – Suma Organic Peeled Tomatoes (AZDA sell good ones, too)
- Sunflower and pumpkin seeds – I buy "Suma" from Archie Browns or "Neil's Yard Whole foods" in 500g bags from my local health shop Holland & Barrett (Suma tastes better though)
- From Holland & Barrett I also buy things like magnesium tablets, moisturizers and flax seeds

I BUY THESE FROM MY LOCAL GROCERIES STORE (SAINSBURY'S):

- You can find the essentials pretty much in any grocery store if you look in their organic/ health food aisle.
- The one closest to me is called SAINSBURY'S. Here's what I buy there on a regular basis:
- Organic brown rice milk – Rice dream original - you can also buy it from the other local groceries store "Tesco"
- Unsweetened almond milk – Alpro - (and I sometimes make my own - mostly I use rice milk though)
- Extra Virgin Olive Oil –Sainsbury's own
- Tomato puree without citric acid (do you say paste?) – Napolina Double Concentrate
- Yeast free Stock Cubes – Kallo or Anthony Worrall's
- Low Sodium Salt – Low Salt
- Good quality still bottled water – Volvic
- Tinned chickpeas -- Napolina
- Tinned fish – I buy John West Tuna in spring water and Sardines in sunflower oil
- Frozen peas – (any that are "freshly frozen"), also frozen fish
- Brown rice – I buy 1kg bags of Sainsbury's Brown or 500g bags of Tilda Wholegrain rice
- Fresh ginger root
- Probiotic yogurt – I buy Woodland Dairy's sheep yogurt (it's creamy and mild just like Greek yogurt)

I BUY THESE ON-LINE:

- Bones for making bone broth – I get beef bone marrow from Riverford home delivery at www.riverford.co.uk and I buy a chicken for roasting pretty much every week, I use the carcass for the broth
- Organic meat – I buy this at Sainsbury's, Tesco's or Riverford and sometimes from a farmer's market
- Organic vegetables and herbs– I get a bi-monthly organic vegetable delivery from Riverford at www.riverford.co.uk (it's more affordable than you think!); then I also buy fresh organic veggies at my local groceries shop

- Dandelion tea – this and other herbal teas I buy at my local health food shop Archie Browns (Nettle, Mullein , Sage and other speciality teas I buy at woodlandherbs.co.uk
- Natural apple cider vinegar – I buy a big bottle of Ostler's from ostlerscidermill.co.uk online or from my local health food shop
- Chia seeds – I buy Organic chia seeds on the internet in 1kg bags -- BuyWholefoodsOnline.com
- Hemp seeds – The Happy Health Company – de-hulled hemp seeds, 1 kg bag – I buy it from Amazon
- Vanilla Stevia drops – NuNaturals from Amazon.co.uk

Remember you can adapt the list to fit your own lifestyle (especially depending on what's available to buy near you and that fits your budget. Don't think you'll have to get everything on this list - it's just meant as guidance.

Hope you'll find this resources/ pantry list useful, and **if you have any questions or additional comments feel free to post them at http://candidadietplan.com/candida-faq/**

Take care, Sandra

PANTRY LIST/ GROCERIES LIST FOR STAGE 1

This list is for 1 person. Remember the idea is to consume mostly vegetable broth for at least 2 days, no solid food. And then follow the recipes for Stage 2.

Ingredients for Fasting Tea:

- 2 sticks cinnamon
- 6 cloves
- 1 tablespoon aniseed (or fennel seeds)
- 1.5l (1.5 quarts or a good 6 US cups) filtered water

Ingredients for Veggy Broth:

- 1.5l filtered water
- 1 handful broccoli
- 1 handful cabbage
- 1 onion
- 2 leeks
- 1 stalk celery
- 2 handfuls kale or spinach
- 2 carrots
- 2 potatoes
- 1-2 yeast free vegetable stock cubes

Ingredients for Green Goodness Juice:

- 1 handful fresh basil or cilantro
- half a large cucumber
- 1-2 celery stalks
- 1 lemon
- Optional : 1 clove garlic, a few tea spoons of spirulina powder & chlorella powder

Ingredients for Tomato & Basil Pick Me Up Juice

- 6 ripe tomatoes on the vine
- 1 handful fresh basil leaves
- a sprinkle salt & freshly ground black pepper
- a sprinkle garlic granules

Other useful ingredients:

- brown rice
- vegetables of your choice e.g. asparagus, broccoli, leek, cabbage, peas, bell peppers, cherry tomatoes, courgettes (zucchinis), avocadoes (as many as you want and think you can eat in 3-7 days!)

Quick Shopping List:

- Olive oil
- Low salt, freshly ground pepper, turmeric and cayenne pepper
- (optional: fennel seeds, aniseed, cloves, cinnamon)
- 2 yeast free stock cubes
- 1 head of white cabbage
- 1 head of broccoli
- 1 big onion
- 4 leeks
- 1 head of celery
- 1 carrot (optional)
- 1 potato (optional)
- 6 handfuls of kale or spinach
- 1 pot fresh basil or cilantro
- 2-4 organic lemons
- 2 large organic cucumbers
- 1 bulb of garlic
- 1 bag of frozen peas
- fresh bunch of asparagus
- 6 or more avocados
- 3 multi colour bell peppers
- 1-2 packs of cherry tomatoes
- Any other vegetables of your choice

Optional:
- spirulina & chlorella powder)
- organic beef or chicken bones for making bone broth

TOP TIP:
Before embarking on the cleanse - Stock up on a few things for the actual diet, too.
Once you are fasting you won't feel like carrying huge bags of groceries around.

Useful Stage 2 ingredients you might want to buy in advance or get freshly delivered are:

- 6 eggs
- 2 fillets of salmon
- 1 whole chicken
- 1 aubergine
- 1 courgette
- 2 red and yellow bell peppers
- can of organic tomatoes
- cinnamon
- coconut oil
- 1 kg bag brown rice

FREQUENTLY ASKED QUESTIONS

Will these recipes/the meal plan work for you?

This meal plan is simply a guideline what your diet could look like. Every Candida Diet is slightly different. So depending if you are a vegan for instance or if you are an athlete or whether you are very ill – you have to adapt your diet accordingly. There is no one size fits all. I have endeavored to incorporate as many healthy eating rules into my plan as possible. So most people with Candida would be absolutely fine with my plan. But if in doubt get a tailor made menu plan from a nutritionist or naturopath.

Why did I include so many meat, egg & fish dishes on my menu?

You might lose quite a bit of weight by following my plan. The extra protein from the meat, eggs and fish gives you energy so you are not tired and ravenous all the time. Just eating veg, apart from not being a complete meal, wouldn't make you feel full for long.

I don't like fish – Can I replace the fish meals with meat?

Technically yes, but I would not recommend it, since eating meat promotes inflammation which is often a problem with Candida sufferers. So if you want to heal fast and particularly if you are quite ill to begin with – make a point of eating lots of fish, even taking fish oil and flax seed oil to help bring your inflammations down. Drinking lots of chamomile tea helps with this, too. Eggs, meat and butter on the other hand promote inflammation. So have less of those when you have any painful, swollen or red areas in your body.

Can I change the amounts of what's on the menu?

Of course you can, these are just examples from me, since I am always hungry and also do quite a bit of physical work and long hours in front of the computer. If you find more time to rest, than it would be appropriate to swap a few meat meals for some lighter veggy options or have smaller portions. I wouldn't necessarily advise you to eat lots more though ;-)

I am a Vegetarian/ Vegan – what are my options?

I hear you! – I am working on a plan to suit your requirements as we speak. I already have the menu suggestions together but not the amounts and recipes directions...

Do I have to stick to this plan religiously?

No, if you have come across some other nourishing anti candida recipes then by all means include them. Likewise if you include or swap certain ingredients that's fine, too; as long as you have ½- ¾ of your plate vegetable/ salad based and 1/3 -1/2 protein based (meat, egg, fish, chickpeas).

Can I eat all the vegetables I want?

Yes and no. All vegetables are good, but some by their very nature are harder to digest than others. Fried onions and garlic for instance are very acidic and can cause stomach upsets in sensitive individuals. Since the goal of this stage of the diet is to minimize digestive upsets you should aim to eat predominantly veggies that are gently on your system, especially if you have a lot of inflammation in your body. Cucumbers and Courgettes (Zucchinis) are excellent *(I know they taste bland - get over it!)*.

Green peppers, aubergines, fennel and leek are good too. Red peppers on the other hand contain more sugar than green ones. So for this Stage of the diet try to stick with green peppers *(even if they don't taste as nice!)*

Are fried foods off the books now?

The way your food or in this case vegetables are prepared makes a bit difference to how you feel and to how quickly you are healing. Frying robs your body of important nutrients and causes acid production - bad news for healing. Cooking is ok. But grilling and steaming are best. So do yourself a favor and grill and steam most of your foods for the next two weeks and whenever you're not feeling well!

What if I skip a meal or a whole day due to a work or family commitment?

Simply follow on from where you left off on the plan or pick a different day to start on again. The order doesn't matter. I just picked this order to make it easier for you to bulk prepare certain meals (like brown rice or soup for 2 days in a row).

What If I have no time to cook a full on meal?

Find a way to make it easier or bulk cook the same meal for several days. For instance I felt too tired to make a salad – so I just ate gem lettuce leaves with my lunch instead.

What if I have no appetite?

Get into the habit of drinking green smoothies; possibly with the addition of protein powder and Chia seeds for extra nourishment. Not eating is not an option -- you need energy for healing!

What if I feel overwhelmed?

Stop whatever it is you're doing and go for a brisk 10 min walk. No time to do that? Then simply lie on your back on the floor for a few minutes with your knees bent (balances your nervous system and is marvelous to combat back ache, seriously ;-)

What if I don't like something on the menu?

Adapt the menu to your requirements and circumstances. For instance if you want to eat butter rather than coconut butter that I use in most my recipes, just adjust the recipe accordingly. If you don't feel like eating meat 2 days in a row, swap some menus out. But make sure you're getting enough protein, otherwise you'll lose muscle mass, get too thin or feel weak.

What if I'm on a budget?

You can get away with using only certain ingredients. You don't have to use them all. I only wanted to give you variety. For instance you don't need to eat chicken one day then turkey the next. It's perfectly fine to have chicken both days or just eat soup without turkey – you get the idea... Try to buy organic meat & veg wherever possible though.

How can I season food if I'm not allowed cheese, cream or similar condiments?

Do you find Candida Diet meals a bit bland? You are not alone! When I started the diet I was surprised how boring and "same old – same old" everything tasted.

No wonder, considering that cheese, cream, soya sauce and most other seasonings (with sugar, malt, citric acid, vinegar…) are off the books while you are fighting Candida.

What you can use for seasoning though is an amino acid blend called **Bragg's Amino liquid**. Another good option is to **use Indian seeds and spices in your cooking. They have a wonderfully invigorating and health boosting effect on your body and are also very flavorsome.** That said, you should use the spices sparingly, only to accentuate.

General Tips for Improved Digestion:

- Drink Fresh Ginger Tea
- Take a good Muti Vit & Mineral Complex
- Take spirulina/ chlorella for extra energy
- Drink apple cider vinegar
- Aim to eat dinner no later than 6.pm
- Eat healthy portions (see Stage 2 guidelines)
- Always eat easy to digest food (carbs e.g. fruit, bread, beans, potatoes, rice, pasta) before heavy food (meat, fish, oily stuff)
- Use good fats like coconut oil and extra virgin olive oil
- Add spices and herbs
- Go for a quick walk morning and evening
- Drink loose nettle/ dandelion tea and mint/ chamomile tea
- Grill, steam or bake your food instead of frying
- Take a power nap after lunch & aim to be in bed by 10.30pm
- Make a point of doing something relaxing & solely enjoyable – more often ;-)

If you liked this book please go to Amazon, and leave a quick rating/ review -- that would really help me in a big way (there are so many Candida books out there, it's easy to go under otherwise...)

ACKNOWLEDGEMENTS

I would like to use this opportunity to thank a few people who helped me get this book out into the world:

My mum and her sister and her brother who all in their own rights are fantastic hobby chefs. I have no doubt I inherited my mum's joy of cooking and baking and the eye for detail, my aunt's creativity and my uncle's way of celebrating and presenting food.

My dad - he loves food as much as I do, and always made sure I had enough to eat, even as a poor student.

Johnny - my partner of 10 years - he not only had to eat his way through most of my unconventional cooking creations. He also saw me change my diet and lifestyle 360 degrees in the past 5 years. When we started going out we used to eat bagels, cheesy sandwiches, sponge cake and have ice cream smoothies together; not to mention one or the other cocktail. These days I get more excited about eating gluten free pancakes than any of the treats we used to enjoy together. Oh and he created the smashing cover for this book and laid out the images, how cool is that!

I'd also like to thank Johnny's mum Jackie, who encouraged me to bake, when I was too anxious to make anything more than a packet soup or pasta, and whose amazing cooking skills inspired me try my luck at cooking myself. Johnny's dad and brother deserve a thanks as well as their loving supportive smiles never left their faces no matter how dry yet another gluten and sugar free cake of mine turned out to be.

Not to forget my amazing taste testers - all the readers who kindly cooked some of my recipes and gave me their honest feedback to make the recipes better.

Thanks also goes to my lovely editor Julie Edmonson who has done a stellar job (yet again!) at clarifying my message.

I would also like to thank Lewis Howes and my buddies in the School of Greatness Academy for feedback, emotional support and for holding me accountable to get this book published.

Last but not least thank YOU for picking up this book - I hope you'll put it to good use ;-)

Enjoyed this read...?

Well, grab the next in the series of the Sugar Free And Easy Candida Diet Recipes. Book 2 contains a whole bunch of hearty (but healthy) comfort foods that will aid you in your journey back to health!

Just search on Amazon for...

Sugar Free And Easy Candida Diet Recipes Book 2

INDEX

Juice (Tomato & Basil Pick me up) 20

K

Kale and Coconut Stir-fry 55

L

Lamb or Beef Bolognese Stew 40

O

Omelet with Green Pepper and Leek 24
Oven Omelet (with veggies and/or bacon) 34

P

Pantry list 65
Poached Cod with Cherry Tomatoes 25

Q

Quiche (with topping of your choice e.g. Leek, Broccoli & Bacon) 36

R

Ratatouille with Coconut Rice 38
Recap of stage 1 20; Recap of stage 2 56
Rice (brown Rice cooked to creamy consistency) 23
Roast Chicken with Red Onion Gravy 39

S

Salad Niçoise (Simple Version of Salad with Tuna & Boiled Egg) 31
Salad with Grilled Chicken 30
Salmon with Greens, Beans & Peas 41
Sardines and Boiled Egg 33
Smoothie (Creamy Green Calmer) 19
Snacks (Stage 2 Protein) 51
Soup (Cauliflower & Almond) 28
Soup (Cavolo Nero/Kale & Roast Meat) 29
Soup (Chicken, Leek & Green Veg) 27
Soup (Creamy Veg with Crispy Turkey Strips) 43
Spicy Chickpeas 54

T, V & Y

Thai Green Curry... delicious & mild! 42
Tomato & Basil Pick me up Juice 20
Tuna or Cooked Turkey minced meat Snack with Gem Lettuce 55
Tuna Steak with Tomato Salsa 44
Vegetable Broth 16
Yogurt with Coconut & Sunflower seeds and nuts sprinkled on the top 48

Cinnamon Coconut Cereal

Makes 2 portions

1 cup desiccated coconut
½ cup sunflower seeds
1 flax egg
Dash almond milk
Handful nuts (macadamias good)
1 tbsp coconut oil, melted
8 drops stevia
Pinch vanilla seeds + sea salt + spices

Oven 180°C. Line a baking sheet w paper
Whizz the seeds + coconut, not too fine
    (can keep back some for added texture).
Add the egg + spices + mix well.
Finely chop the nuts + stir into the mix.

Scoop onto the tray, + flatten w a spatula
Mark into 2cm squares w a wet knife

Bake 15-30 mins. Cool + break into □'s.
Keep in fridge or freeze. Can crumble up
    + use as a crumble topping.

Almond Butter Dough Balls

20g / ¼ cup desiccated coconut
50g / ½ cup almond butter
30g / ¼ cup coconut flour
4 tbsp plant milk
1-2 drops stevia
1 tbsp coconut oil

Mix in a food processor, adding more
    butter or flour if it is too crumbly/wet

Roll into balls. Keep in fridge.

Printed in Great Britain
by Amazon.co.uk, Ltd.,
Marston Gate.